Doing the Impossible!

God Manifesting His Supernatural Power through You!

Part 2

Rudi Louw

Table of Contents

The Marvel of the Holy Bible

1. Uninterrupted Theme and Inspired Thought

It took *1,500 years* to compile the Holy Bible, involving *more than 40 different authors*. <u>Yet</u> the theme and inspired thought of Scripture continues *uninterrupted* from author to author, from beginning till end.

2. Absence of Mythical Stories

Compare philosophies and theories about creation in the Middle East, Europe, Asia, Africa, and Latin America and you'll find mythical scenarios: gods feuding and cutting up other gods to form the heavens and the earth, etc.

In ancient Greek mythology, the Greeks see Atlas carrying the earth on his shoulders. In India, Hindus believe eight elephants carry the earth on their backs.

But in contrast, Job, the oldest book in the Holy Bible, declares that, *"God suspends the earth on nothing."* (Job 26:7)

This was said millennia before Isaac Newton discovered the invisible laws of gravity that delicately balance every planet and sun in its individual circuit.

Contrary to every other ancient attempt to give a creation account, *the Holy Bible pictures the creation of the earth in a very scientific manner.*

For example, in Genesis Chapter One, the continents are lifted from the seas, then vegetation is formed and later animal life, all reproducing *'according to its own kind',* **thus recognizing the fixed genetic laws.** In addition, we have the bringing forth of man and woman, *all done by God in a dignified and proper manner, without mythological adornments.*

The balance or remainder of the Holy Bible follows suite.

The narratives are **true historical documents**, *faithfully reflecting society and culture* **as history and archaeology would discover them thousands of years later. Not only is the Holy Bible historically accurate, it is also reliable when it deals with scientifically proven subjects.**

It was never intended to be a textbook on history, science, mathematics, or medicine. *However, when its writers touch on these subjects,* **they often state facts that scientific advancement would not reveal, or**

6

even consider, until thousands of years later.

While many have doubted the accuracy of the Holy Bible, time and continued research have consistently demonstrated that the Word of God is better informed than its critics.

3. Intactness

Of all the ancient works of substantial size, *the Holy Bible survives intact, against all odds and expectations.*

Compared with other ancient writings, the Holy Bible has more manuscripts as evidence to support it than any ten pieces of classical literature combined!

The plays of William Shakespeare, for instance, were written about four hundred years ago, after the invention of the printing press. Many of his original writings and words have been lost in numerous sections, *yet the Holy Bible's uncanny preservation has weathered thousands of years of wars, contradictions, persecutions, fires and invasions.*

Through the centuries Jewish scribes have preserved the Holy Bible's Old Covenant text, ***such as no other manuscripts have ever been preserved****. **They kept tabs on every letter, syllable, word and paragraph**. They* *continued from generation to generation to appoint and train special groups of men within their culture* **whose sole duty it was to preserve and transmit these documents <u>with perfect accuracy and fidelity</u>.**

Who ever bothered to count the letters, syllables, or words of Plato, Aristotle, or Seneca for that matter?

When it comes to the New Testament, the actual number of preserved manuscripts is so great that it becomes overwhelming**.** ***There are more than 5,680 Greek manuscripts, more than 10,000 Latin Vulgate manuscripts and at least 9,300 other versions. Further still, there exists an additional 25,000 manuscript copies of portions of the New Testament.*** **No other document of antiquity even begins to approach such numbers.**

The closest in comparison is Homer's <u>Iliad</u>, with only 643 manuscripts. The first complete work of Homer only dates back to the 13th century.

4. Unmatched Accuracy in Predictive Foretelling

The Holy Bible is unmatched in accuracy in predictive foretelling. .No other ancient work succeeds in this, or even begins to attempt this.

Other books such as the Koran, the Book of Mormon, and parts of the Veda claim divine inspiration; ***but none of these books contain predictive foretelling.***

This one undeniable fact we know for certain: *While microscopic scrutiny would show up the imperfections, blemishes, and defects of any work of man, <u>it magnifies the beauties and perfection of God</u>. Just as every flower displays in accurate detail the reflection and perfection of beauty, <u>so does the Word of Truth when it is scrutinized</u>.*

Historian Philip Schaff wrote:

*"Without money and weapons, Jesus the Christ conquered more millions than Alexander, Caesar, Mohammad, and Napoleon. Without science and learning, He (Jesus the Christ) shed more light on things human and divine than all philosophers and scholars combined. Without the eloquence of schools, He (Jesus the Christ) spoke such words of life as was never spoken before or since and produced effects which lie beyond the reach of orator or poet. Without writing a single line, He (Jesus the Christ) set more pens in motion and furnished themes for more sermons, orations, discussions, learned volumes, works of art, and songs of praise **than the whole army of great men of ancient and modern times combined**." (The Person of Christ*, p33. 1913)

Today, there are literally billions of Bibles in more than 2,000 languages.

Isn't it about time you find out what it really has to say?

Hey listen, the Holy Bible is all about Jesus, the Messiah, the Christ…

…and everything about Jesus Christ is really about YOU!!

Study Tips:

Read 2 Corinthians 5:14, 16, 18, 19, and 21.

In the light of these Scriptures, it should be obvious that, if you want to study the Holy Bible, *you should study it in the light of Mankind's redemption!*

Feed daily on **redemption realities** found in the book of Acts, in Romans Chapters One through Eight, and in Ephesians, Colossians, and Galatians. These realities may also be found in 1 Peter Chapter One, 2 Peter Chapter One, James Chapter 1, as well as in 1 and 2 Corinthians.

Foreword

Thank you for taking the time to read this book.

Let me start off by saying that *I am totally addicted to my Daddy's love for me.*

I am in love with Jesus Christ, *and that is enough for me!*

The love of God is so much more than a doctrine, a philosophy, or a theory. It is so much more and goes so much deeper than knowledge; it way surpasses knowledge. *We are talking heart language here.*

I write *to impact people's hearts,* to make them see the mysteries that have been hidden in Father God's heart concerning Christ Jesus, and actually *concerning THEM,* so as to arrest their conscience with it, *that I may introduce them to their original design and to their true selves,* **and present them to themselves perfect in Christ Jesus** *and set them apart unto Him* **in love,** as a chaste virgin.

We are involved with the biggest romance of the ages. Therefore this book cannot be read as you would a novel: *casually.* It is not a cleverly devised little myth or fable. **It contains revelation and** *truth* **into some things you may or may not have considered before.**

It is not blasphemy or error though. *It is the TRUTH of God, ultimate TRUTH, and therefore has direct bearing upon YOUR life.* The Word and the Spirit are my witness *to the reality of these things!*

Be like the people of Berea the apostle Paul ministered to in Acts 17:11. Open yourself up to study the revelation contained in this book ***to discover for yourself the reality of these things***.

*Be forewarned! Do not become guilty of the sins of the Pharisees, **or you too will miss out on the depth of fulfillment God Himself, who is LOVE, wants to give you***.

Jesus said of the Pharisees and Sadducees that they strain out every little gnat BUT swallow whole camels. What He meant by that is that *some people seem to have it all together when it comes to doctrine and they love to argue. **It makes them feel important, but it is nothing other than EMPTY religious and intellectual pride.** They know the Scriptures in and out, and YET they are still so IGNORANT about **REAL TRUTH that is only found in LOVE.** They are still so ignorant and indifferent **towards the things that REALLY MATTER**. They are always arguing over the use of every little jot and tittle and over the meaning and interpretation of every word of Scripture.*

The exact thing they accuse everyone else of doing though, the precise thing they judge everyone else for, *they are actually doing themselves.* That is **they often downright misinterpret and twist what is being said, *making a big deal of insignificant things while obscuring or weakening God's real truth: the truth of His LOVE*.** *They are always majoring on minors* **<u>because they do not understand the heart of God</u> and therefore they constantly miss the whole point of the message**.

Paul himself said it so beautifully,

*"…the letter kills but **the Spirit BRINGS LIFE**;"*

*"…<u>knowledge puffs up</u>, but **LOVE EDIFIES**."*

I say again:

Allow yourself to get caught up in the revelation I am about to share. Open yourself up to study the insight contained in this book, *not only with a desire to gain knowledge, but also with anticipation **to hear from Father God yourself**;*

…to encounter Him through His Word;

*…**and to embrace truth, in order to know and believe the LOVE God has for <u>you</u>**, so that you may get so caught up in it, **that you too may receive from Him LOVES' impartation of LIFE.***

This revelation contains within it the voice and call of LOVE Himself to every human being on the face of this earth. *If you take heed to it, it is custom designed and guaranteed to forever alter and enrich your life!*

Acknowledgment

I want to acknowledge and thank one of my mentors in the faith, Francois du Toit, for blessing and impacting me with revelation knowledge.

I borrowed the portion on *"The Marvel of the Holy Bible"* from his website: http://www.MirrorWord.net, as students so often feel they have a right to do with things that come from teachers they respect. Just as Galatians 6:6 says, *"Let him who is taught the Word **share in all good things** with him who teaches."*

To all our dear friends and family, for all the love and support, and to all those who helped me with this project:

THANK YOU!

Also, especially to my wife, Carmen;

For keeping me real by being my companion in life and partner in ministry,

I love and appreciate you so very much!

"I will not leave you desolate; **I will come to you** ...the world will see Me no more, **but you will see Me.**"

"In that day **you will know** that I am in my Father, **and you in Me, and I in you.**"

"He who treasures my Word (the truth of My gospel), it is he who truly loves Me;"

"...and he who loves Me will be loved by My Father equally,"

"...and I, in My love for him, will manifest Myself to him."

"My Father also will demonstrate His love for him, and We will come to him and make Our home with him."

-John 14:18-23

Chapter 1

Awaken To More!

I just recently had to get me a new Bible, because the old one was falling apart, but I ended up having to constantly go back and forth between the two Bibles for a while, because I had some notes in the old one that I do not yet have in the new one. Those notes and revelations which I received from the Holy Spirit are so precious to me and form the very foundation of thought and faith I build my life upon. But praise God, the Holy Spirit reminded me that that which He has deposited in me is in me whether I have all the notes and references transferred to my new Bible or not... ha... ha... ha...

All that really matters is that we keep receiving the ingredient of truth which God has invested in His word so that it may also be deposited in our spirits! God wants us to make it our business to embrace His truth fully in our hearts!

Listen; a raindrop would mean absolutely nothing to the soil if it does not contain the nutrients and all the moisture the soil needs to sprout forth new life.

That is exactly the thing that also makes the Word of God precious; it's not the Scriptures themselves, it's not the printed page, it's not what color ink is used; you know, *'I've got a Red Letter Addition,'* or, *'I've got a commentary written by So-and-so, and I have a special commentary on this and that, and you just have a regular old black letter Bible with no commentary at all,'* **but it is the truth that God deposits inside the Scriptures, inside the gospel contained there, inside His Word** that becomes revelation to us as we embrace it and we make it our own, and we mean business with it, saying to God within ourselves, *'God, we are not taking anything at face value, and we refuse to take Your revealed truth for granted, **because we know that You have granted unto us all things that pertain to life and Godliness through it!** So, whatever You grant to us in revelation, Father, because You have already granted it to us in all reality, in Christ Jesus, **we are determined to possess it fully and make it our own!'***

And so, in reading this book I hope you too are determined to do just that as we fellowship together around His Truth as it is revealed in the Scriptures, and as we just embrace His truth afresh in our hearts and lives again.

As I was writing Part 1 of this series called: *'Doing The Impossible'* I really felt the confirmation of God in my spirit as to the value of this subject and the necessity of this revelation the Holy Spirit desires to lead us all into in the body of Christ.

Listen, it is with absolute conviction that I can say to you that God has more in mind than the ordinary for each and every believer, because He is not an ordinary God. He is not a God that is the product of Man's imagination. He is not an idol that can be compared to the rest of them. He is an extra ordinary God. He is the Great and Mighty One; the Almighty God, amen, and we worship Him! We give Him praise and honor and applause; we esteem Him greatly, we magnify Him in our hearts, amen! **This great and mighty GOD desires for each and every one of His children to live an extra ordinary life; to live the life of the supernatural, and not to be limited to just an ordinary existence.**

Listen; He has more in mind for you than the daily hum drum and routine of an existence centered around mere survival in the natural on this planet.

I really do believe that God has a life full of the miraculous in mind for each and every person who has grasped the fact that they are indeed the sons of God.

The Scriptures are not an instruction book for us to just kind of make it, to just kind of keep our heads above the water and to just sort of live and barely rise above our problems in a small meager measure, but God's Word, the gospel, made known there in the Scriptures, guarantees the life of the overcomer to the believer. God says that we are more than conquerors. God wants our lives daily to testify of victory upon victory upon victory, amen, I really believe this!

God doesn't intend for any of us to live in the frustration of defeat, and the frustration of just not being able to make ends meet, and just not quite being able to live that life more abundantly He had in mind for us from the beginning!

I say again, the Scriptures are not an instruction book for us to just kind of make it in life, no it is a book written in order to break open new revelation for us into our sonship; **it's an instruction book into our sonship in order for us to be able to lay a hold of our full inheritance as children of God!**

In the truth of the gospel, in the knowledge of Him revealed, God truly has provided for us every ingredient that we need to enjoy His fullness.

And so in this book you hold in your hand I want us to allow the Holy Spirit, as our one and only Teacher, as the One who reveals the deep things of the heart of God to those who search these things out and longs to intimately know them, to come and instruct us.

I yield to You Holy Spirit, as an instrument would yield to its Master I yield to You, to use my mind and inspire my thoughts and my spirit, to communicate through my fingers, just as the pen of a ready writer would inscribe a message upon the hearts of its readers, I ask You Holy Spirit **to quicken life within the hearts and minds of those who read these books, not as skeptics and cynics, but as believers.**

In Jesus Name

Amen

Chapter 2

God Is No Respecter Of Persons!

In Part 1 of this series we looked at Mary's encounter with the Word of God. John 1:1 says, *"In the beginning was the Word."* You see Mary's encounter was with *that* Word. Her encounter in the first place was not with an angel. Would you agree with me on that? Her encounter was with the Word of God, just as John 1:14 says, *"The Word became flesh and dwelt within us."* Mary was privileged to have the experience of that Word embraced by her, *conceiving within her womb and supernaturally taking upon itself flesh, and manifesting itself* in the birth of that child in a physical body.

In Luke 1 we see how Mary *embraced* that Word that came to her and responded and said, *"Let it be to me according to Your Word."*

The angel greeted her with the favor of God and said: *"Hail to you, O favored one!"* And so we considered in Part 1 what motivates God's favor towards Mary, or anyone else for that matter, because God is no respecter of persons. I mean, He showed Mary favor while she was still under the Law, but really it was because He favored her with the favor that was already in His heart towards the whole human race. That favor towards us has been in His heart from the beginning and resides there permanently, in spite of the fall.

In Romans Chapter 2:11 and in other verses Paul makes it plain that God shows no partiality. God is no respecter of persons. God does not esteem one person over another. But God has a genuine love inside of Him for every human being, and therefore a burning desire within His heart, for every single one of us to come into the full knowledge of our sonship and our absolute salvation revealed in Jesus Christ.

So, whatever it was in the heart of God that drew Him to Mary is the exact same thing that draws Him to you also!

It is called grace!

As far is God is concerned you already have His favor! You are indeed blessed and highly favored!

Ephesians 1:3 clearly says that, *"He has blessed you with every possible blessing that heaven could possibly contain."*

He blessed us with Himself!

Listen, God has already blessed us with Himself, in Christ Jesus!

In blessing us with Himself, with His person, with His favor, *He has already blessed us with everything.*

There is therefore nothing left for God to bless us with that He has not already blessed us with when He blessed us with Himself!

That is what that word, "grace" represents: The very fullness of God; the full content of His heart – His love in abundance!

When we have Him we have everything!

"And of His fullness have we all received; grace in abundance - beyond measure!" - John 1:16

His fullness is our portion in Christ Jesus!

In this book I want to focus on things that accompany the gospel, but in order for you to more fully understand the gospel, you really should get and read some of my other books in which I expound more fully on the grace of God and focus more acutely on what the gospel really is, like *"God's Love For You!" - "God's Inheritance In You!" - "God's Eternal Purpose" - "Offspring of God" - "You Are Innocent!" and "Fully Persuaded".*

Listen we truly do not receive anything from God through the works of the Law! God does not reward us based on our diligence in keeping the Law!

You see Mary had to really consider in her heart the kind of greeting she was greeted with by the angel, because the Jewish mentality in Mary's world was educated to relate to God in terms of Moses; on the terms of the Law, and so they, brainwashed by that prevailing mindset, knew that none were righteous through the Law. They knew that even their best sinned and transgressed. They knew that even their High Priest was a sinner who failed often; not even the High Priest was righteous under the Law. They knew that not even the High Priest could quite make it in relationship with God, because he had to continually offer guilt and shame sacrifices. That same blood which he offered for the sins of the people he had to first offer for his own sins (Hebrews 5:3 & Hebrews 7:27).

Even today still many religious people try to relate to God in terms of Moses or Mohammad or whomever; on the terms of the Law, on the terms of their own particular brand of religious Law and obligations and expectations, and so just like the Jews of old, *their relationship to God is always one of feeling slightly condemned and feeling guilty towards Him.*

But I thank God that when suddenly the voice of God came and interrupted that religious mindset and confronted that prevailing religious mentality within Mary when He greeted her with His favor and with His eternal purpose which originated in His grace, she responded by not only considering it in her heart and noting the contrast, but she embraced the gospel greeting of God in preference to her own religious Jewish mentality!

I say again: We truly do not receive anything from God through the works of the Law; God really does not reward us based on our diligence in keeping the Law (obeying the obligations of our religion, whether we are Christian, Muslim, Hindu or whatever), but He responds to us and interacts with us solely on the grounds of the gospel of grace.

God's message to the Law-minded is: *'I relate to you and respond positively to you, not based on the merits of your own performance and achievement under the Law within your particular religion,* **but based on My grace demonstrated in Jesus Christ; based on the grounds of My own diligence on your behalf in the Son. That Son, Jesus, became obedient to the point of shedding His own blood on your behalf. He became obedient and together We took upon Ourselves your supposed punishment.**

See fulfilled in Him your punishment; *that image of your deserved punishment* **conjured up in your own minds eye,** *as projected onto your imagination by the Law within your religion and its ministry and message of death.'*

You see the works of the Law represents our failure or our achievement in keeping the Law,

but the grace of God demonstrated in Jesus represents Gods achievement in Him.

So therefore Gods relationship with Man as revealed in the new Covenant is based not upon Man's achievement, not upon Man's ability or inability to keep the Law, but **it is based on the Godheads success in Jesus Christ.**

In Him They conquered sin and destroyed the works of the Devil when Jesus entered into and suffered our hell.

And now, hallelujah, through that resurrection life, through that newness of life we have our grounds for ministry!

So now let us get to our subject which I really want to get to in this book. Paul, in Galatians 2:5 asks, *"He who works mighty works within us and among us; He who brings a supernatural witness to the reality of spirit dimension and of spirit-truth among us, does He work those works because we somehow earn the right to receive those manifestations through our diligence in keeping the Law, or does God do those works through our hearing with faith?"*

Paul goes on to say that *"He does it solely through our hearing with faith!"*

Listen: **When we finally have ears to hear what the Spirit of God is *truly* saying to us in Jesus Christ we qualify not only for the**

supernatural experience of a lifetime, but also for a lifetime of experiencing the supernatural and the miraculous.

I truly do believe that God desires to tangibly witness to the reality of the resurrection of Jesus Christ and its impact as far as the human race is concerned!

God desires to bring witness to that resurrection power through signs and wonders and through the supernatural becoming evident in the assembly of the believers and in the ordinary lives of the people of faith.

As we get together and as we begin to praise Him and enter into praise of Him ourselves personally, **we begin to witness the very presence of God, and we know that in the experience of His nearness there is an immediate opportunity for the Holy Spirit to manifest in power.**

I Corinthians 12:7 says that *"The manifestation of the Holy Spirit is given to all, for the benefit of all."*

In my 30 some years of involvement in church and in ministry I have seen this often enough in our meetings and in my own life as well: Even if I am in the middle of buying groceries at Wall-Mart, *the minute I become aware in my own spirit of the nearness of God,* **an environment** is created which is *immediately conducive to the supernatural and the miraculous.*

I repeat; I have seen it often enough to have learned this: **As soon as the manifestation of the Holy Spirit becomes evident** in the meeting or even just in your own spirit as you are engaged in normal life activities, **get ready for the supernatural and miraculous to manifest; get ready for the gifts of the Spirit to operate.**

Hey, the manifestation of the Holy Spirit within your spirit does not just happen in order to entertain us; He is not just here to help us have a nice time experiencing God's nearness in our spirit and whenever we gather together and have our meetings! I thank God for that, but listen, **the Holy Spirit is also here and manifests Himself within our spirit t***o manifest the glory and the presence and the power of God within our midst and through us!*

1 Corinthians 12:4-11 very clearly talks about the supernatural manifestation and enabling of the Holy Spirit that is given to **all** for the sake of ministering to others; demonstrating the very presence and glory and power of God.

In 1 Corinthians 14:1 Paul goes as far as to say: *"Pursue love **and desire** spiritual gifts."*

In verse 12 he says: *"Since you are indeed zealous for spiritual gifts, let it be for the edification of others* (not yourself) *that you seek to excel in these things."*

This enabling; these gifts are not given to us per se, so we can boast about having them, no, these gifts, this supernatural enabling by the Holy Spirit are given for those who are in need of ministry. The Holy Spirit merely enables us to distribute these gifts to the ones who need to be ministered to.

I say again: These are the gifts of the Holy Spirit. These are not our gifts. They do not belong to us per se. They belong to the Holy Spirit who lives in us and manifests Himself within us and through us. We are co-workers together with God, and the Holy Spirit distributes these gifts to enable us to minister to the needs of people.

I want you to notice that Paul does not say that one gift in particular is to be desired above all other gifts. Why? Because people's needs are not the same.

Paul said in 1 Corinthians 12:31, *"But earnestly desire* **the best gifts,** *(the ones that are most needed at the time of ministry; the ones that are most helpful)* **and yet I show you a more excellent way."** He was talking about the way of love, the very *"agape"* - the very love of God Himself, the grace of God Himself, manifesting and flowing out to others from within us.

All of 1 Corinthians 13 was written and dedicated to emphasize the way of love; this agape, this love-nature of God that is within us and wants to manifest through us and flow out of us. Those who care; those who genuinely love people and want to help them in their needs gets supernaturally enabled by the Holy Spirit to do so. **That's what the gifts of the Spirit is all about; it's about the very presence and love and power and glory of God abiding in us and manifesting through us!**

You see when Paul was talking about **pursuing love <u>and</u> desiring spiritual gifts to manifest** (1 Corinthians 14:1) he was talking about a desire that is born out of love.

You see God not only loves us, **He is love.** We need to understand that God **is** love. The essence of God is **love**. Therefore the essence of faith is **love**, and the essence of the anointing is **love**. The essence of our supernatural enabling by the Holy Spirit is **love**! The essence of the anointing, the substance of it; what gives it substance is **love**.

God is love and we are partakers of His divine nature. We are children of God; the very offspring of God, therefore we are love children of a love God, and the love of God is in us and that love wants to be released to flow through us.

Love wants to find expression in you!

Hallelujah!

Faith works by love!

All the gifts of the Spirit come out of love!

Whether it is prophecy, a word of wisdom, a word of knowledge, other tongues, interpretation of other tongues, discerning of spirits, miracles, or various kinds of healing, *it is done through faith, **but it all flows out of love.***

Love has to be our motive, *because faith only works through love.*

Let me get back to what I was saying, before I totally get off tract here... ha... ha... ha...

Chapter 3

How Do We Enter In?

We really need to begin to understand the favor of God.

You see when Mary was greeted with the truth of the gospel in Luke 1 and then was told that the Word will take on flesh in her womb, and that she shall be with child, **that revelation infused her with faith; with a vision inspired by the gospel itself,** and thus prompted her faith response of amazement: *"How shall this be for I have no husband"* She wasn't questioning and doubting the Word, no, *she was amazed and filled with expectation,* **she knew that the experience she was about to enter into was going to be supernatural;** it was not going to be the result of the natural. The angel confirmed this, he answered and said: *"The Holy Spirit will overshadow you..."*

Now I don't know about you, but I desire to live a life that exists under the shadow of the Almighty; I desire to live my life in the shadow of the Holy Spirit, or *being overshadowed by the Holy Spirit* is a better way of putting it. I mean, I desire to live in such a conscious awareness of the Holy Spirit's presence that His shadow marks my every conversation; that when I open my lips to speak that there will be a strong witness to the overshadowing influence of the Holy Spirit. When I conduct my affairs throughout the day, I desire that those affairs will bear witness to the overshadowing of the Holy Spirit, *so that He is the evidence, the evident One in my life.*

The invisible God becomes visible in the flesh through the overshadowing of the Holy Spirit.

He is the One who moves upon people so they may speak from God and act and do as God's true representatives.

Mary said to the angel: *"Let it be unto me according to your Word,"* and we all know how it affected her life and what followed; what happened in her and to her and through her.

2 Timothy 2:15 also talks about *"rightly discerning the Word of God."* You see; **rightly discerning the gospel of God, the truth of that gospel is the only way to enter into the supernatural. The truth of the Gospel; revelation into that truth, always precedes the supernatural.**

Even in Jesus' own life and ministry there in Matthew 9:35 we read how *"He went about and He taught and he preached and He healed."*

Through the proclamation of the gospel, and through His teaching of that Word, He introduced to the people fresh revelation into
38

the truth of the gospel and brought understanding into the minds of the people concerning it and concerning God their Father.

So, *"He went about and He taught and he preached and He healed."*

Can you see how the truth of the gospel being made know preceded the supernatural healing manifestation of God's power?!

If you desire spiritual gifts; if you earnestly desire to walk in the supernatural, if you desire to witness the extra ordinary in your own life you need to learn to escape sin-consciousness and how to deal with feelings of guilt and unworthiness and inferiority, in other words *you need to grasp the content of the gospel accurately,* because **It is impossible to live in the supernatural; to walk in the extra ordinary while you walk feeling condemned and feeling unworthy and feeling that such things couldn't happen with you and that they are beyond you.**

Hey listen; you have had enough law and religion and obligation screamed at you. You need to be greeted with the gospel of Jesus Christ. You need a real revelation of the true gospel of Jesus Christ. **Because in Christ Jesus you were openly forgiven of all your iniquity and there in Him God demonstrated that He does not hold you condemned!**

Praise God for His favor!

Let's go back to 2 Timothy 2:14. The second part of that verse encourages us to *"avoid disputing about words."* He says that *"such disputing does no good; it only leads to the ruin of the hearers. But as for you,"* he says, *"Do your best to present yourself to God **as one already approved,** a workman who has no need to be ashamed, **rightly handling the Word of Truth;** (the truth of the gospel.)"*

In 2 Corinthians 4:2 Paul talks about refusing to practice craftiness; refusing to tamper with the truth of the Gospel. You see the secret of walking in the supernatural lies in rightly handling the truth of the gospel and not tampering with that Word, because Jeremiah 1:12 makes it clear that *"God watches over His Word to perform it and to confirm it!"*

If you were to read that phrase: *"Rightly handling the Word of Truth"* in the original Greek language it speaks of **cutting a straight line, or staying on point, towing the line and not veering off of it, to the left or to the right. It also speaks of cutting straight through distracting arguments and nonsense in order to get the truth straight and sticking to the heart of what is being communicated.**

It speaks of a careful cultivation of truth in order to get the maximum benefit from it.

It is just like a farmer who methodically and carefully plows his field and cuts that furrow in a straight line so that he may get the maximum harvest from that field through his proper measuring; his accurate measuring and careful cultivation of that soil.

So, the Holy Spirit through this passage of scripture encourages us that when we are dealing with the truth of the gospel, we need to discern the truth accurately and be conscious of the fact that we are not just playing around with words, we are not just dealing with mere man-made words and philosophies, but we are dealing with God's Word, with the truth of it, with the true gospel.

In 1st Timothy the author declares emphatically that **every word of God is <u>sure</u>; every word of God is guaranteed.** That means that if we want to begin to rightly discern the truth and power Invested in the gospel, then we first need to discover that the gospel represents the integrity and the guarantee of Gods character and person, and of Gods purpose with Man.

Listen, God is not limited in His purpose. Jesus could easily speak to the stones and they could turn into bread, but He didn't. There is nothing impossible with God. But we read that there is also nothing impossible with him who believes. The understanding of these things and the laying a hold of them have evaded and haunted many a Christian for eons.

So, how do we receive the fullness of the Spirit of God? How do we enter into that realm of living that is above the ordinary?

It is only through the hearing of faith; through the accurate understanding and full embrace of the truth of the gospel!

There is no other way!

Listen, we cannot buy that power.

Man would do anything for power; he would pay any price for the supernatural.

But it doesn't come that way; **it comes through revelation knowledge, through accurate insight and understanding into the truth of the gospel _with a pure heart; with a believing heart,_ and no other way.**

It can only be accessed through faith _inspired by the love of God quickened in our understanding and in our hearts_.

Chapter 4

Simon The Magician

Remember in Acts chapter eight how Simon the magician, who manipulated people out of their money for a living, through His trickery, how he, when he saw how the Holy Spirit came, sought to buy from the apostles the ability to get people filled with the Spirit.

Let's just read it there, starting in Acts 8:9

"There was a man named Simon who previously practiced magic in the city and amazed the people of Samaria with his tricks. He claimed that he was somebody great."

You see there is a difference between employing magic tricks; practicing deception, *and coming with true signs and wonders that is of the Spirit.*

There is a big difference.

When signs and wonders are done in the power of the Spirit, the glory goes to God, straight away. But when you are involved with little games and tricks and gimmicks it is always the magician himself that wants to get the glory.

Verse 10,

"They all gave heed to him from the least to the greatest."

How is that for gaining notoriety? How's that for ministry impact? Oops, I mean, entertainment impact. I was surprised that it wasn't Peter or John or one of the other apostles of notoriety... ha... ha... ha... No I'm just kidding, or am I? Actually, I'm not, it is sad really how many big shot apostles of today act. But it wasn't the apostles of that day, it was a deceiver named Simon who acted that way, amen.

"They all gave heed to him from the least to the greatest, saying, 'This man is the great power of God.' And they all paid attention to him and were manipulated by him, because for a long time now he had amazed and bewitched them with his sorcery; with his practice of magic."

Now verse 12 talks about the impact of Philip's ministry in Samaria, and I want us to study this character Philip in another chapter, but let's just first finish taking a look at Simon the magician.

Verse 12 says,

"But when they believed Philip as he preached the good news about the kingdom of God and the name of Jesus Christ, they were baptized, both men and women."

Philip had revelation about the kingdom of God and about the name of Jesus Christ, and that then was the ingredients of his message, and the Greek language says that, *"they were immersed both men and women."*

Now up to this point Simon had that whole town under his influence; under His control and demand, but when they believed Philip, the hold that Simon had over them was broken.

Verse 13 goes on to say,

"Even Simon himself believed, and after going through the motions of baptism he stuck close to Philip, befriended him and continued with him on his ministry mission through town. And observing the signs and great miracles performed, he was amazed as well."

Simon was a trickster; he was the guy with a trick up his sleeve that was always ready with a new trick, but now he suddenly saw things that absolutely amazed him, but his scheming heart hadn't seen anything yet, and he was about to get the shock of his life, because you may be able to fool everyone else, even your own heart sometimes, but you can't fool God and pull the wool over His eyes. He sees right through you and knows where your heart is at.

Look at this, verse 14,

"Now when the apostles at Jerusalem heard that Samaria had received the Word of God, they sent to them Peter and John, who came

*down and prayed for them that they too might receive the indwelling Holy Spirit; for as of yet He had not fallen upon (the Greek says: **ignited**) any of them, but they had only been immersed in water in the name of the Lord Jesus."*

I want you to notice that there is an important truth that we can clearly see and glean and learn from in this scripture: Obviously Philip did not bring these people into the fullness of that immersion by the Holy Spirit from within. Obviously Philip only introduced these people to the gospel and brought them to a place of faith in Jesus Christ and His completed work of redemption to bring about their salvation.

But when the church over in Jerusalem heard the report about this ministry going on in Samaria, they also knew that although preaching the gospel was a good thing and much was being accomplished there through the ministry of Philip, *there still was a missing dimension to what was happening there.*

The apostles knew that it was wonderful that these people who once followed Simon embraced the gospel and was now following Jesus Christ through the preaching of Philip, *but they were missing out still, there was more for them to experience, there awaited them still another dimension of living, a greater spirit dimension than what they had even entered into up to this point,* and so the church in Jerusalem sent unto them Peter and John, *"who came down and prayed for them that they too might receive the indwelling Holy Spirit; for He had not yet fully revealed Himself and ignited any of them with His presence and passion supernaturally from within, but they had only been immersed in water as an outward sign that they associated themselves with the message and name of the Lord Jesus."*

This scripture very clearly cuts across a few doctrines that say, *'Well, it all happens at the same time. You don't need more than one experience, or a deeper supernatural experience!'*

Listen God intends for us to have the same supernatural experience in the Spirit as the apostles did in Jerusalem in Acts 2, and as these people did in Samaria, and as those 12 guys did whom Paul ran into in Acts 19.

If it takes more than one experience to come into the fullness of the Holy Spirit, and to unlock what needs to be fully unlocked in my inner being, to access and live in the supernatural, then I say, *'Bring it on Holy Spirit, I want it all!'*

And I am not even going to limit His blessing to some so called *'Second Blessing'* either. *'I don't just want a second blessing, I want a third and a fourth and a hundredth blessing, Holy Spirit!'*

I just want His blessings to flow, amen!

I believe that God intends for us to experience Him daily, **to even have an ongoing experience** with Him in the supernatural dimension of the spirit.

The Greek word: ekxeo, **to pour out**, comes to mind. **The Holy Spirit is an outpouring from within, not an in-pouring from without!**

Titus 3:6 in the Mirror Bible says that *"the Holy Spirit is the extravagant Administrator of the salvation of Jesus Christ; **He gushes forth in our midst like an artesian well.**"*

An artesian well is a well sunk through solid strata of sedimentary rock into strata from an area of a higher altitude than that of the well, *so that there is sufficient pressure to force water to flow upwards.* From the French word, artesian, referring to the old French province Artois, where such wells were common.

In John 7:37-39 John records how Jesus witnessed the eighth day, the great and final day of the Feast of Tabernacles, when, according to custom, the High Priest would draw water from the Pool of Siloam with a golden jar, mix the water with wine, and then pour it over the altar while people would sing with great joy from Psalm 118:25-26, and also Isaiah 12:3; *"Therefore with joy shall we draw water from the wells of salvation!"* Then Jesus, knowing that He is the completeness of every prophetic picture and promise, cried out with a loud voice: *"If anyone is thirsty, let him come* *to Me and drink! If you believe that I am what the scriptures are all about, you will discover that you are what I am all about, **and rivers of living waters will gush from your innermost being!**"*

Romans 5:5 also quoted from the Mirror Bible makes it clear that *"**the gift of the Holy Spirit completes our every expectation and ignites the love of God within us like an artesian well.**"*

So here in Acts 8:14 Peter and John wanted those Samaritans not to miss out on the full experience of that reality. They didn't want any of these believers to miss out on the supernatural. They wanted these believers to experience the supernatural as part of their daily lives because of the infilling of the Holy Spirit; the immersion, the indwelling reality and presence of the holy Spirit.

They wanted these believers to experience the extra ordinary, the supernatural, on a consistent bases in their lives, *and not just because Philip is in town and the Holy Spirit has anointed Philip to do signs and wonders and miracles.*

So, *"Peter and John, came down and prayed for them that they too might receive the immersion in the Holy Spirit; for as of yet He had not fallen upon any of them, but they had only been baptized in the name of the Lord Jesus."*

I like that word *"fallen,"* ha... ha... ha...

Listen do not be surprised when people get prayed for and they fall to the ground under the power of God.

When you get totally immersed in the Holy Spirit and His presence and power begins to overwhelm you and overpower your scenes your knees become weak and give way, because it is an intensified concentration of the power and presence of God Himself that enters your spirit and immerses your spirit from out of that unseen spirit dimension of heaven.

It's an outpouring from within, *not an in-pouring from without, amen!*

"Peter and John, prayed for them that they too might receive the immersion in the Holy Spirit; **for as of yet He had not fallen upon (ignited from within) any of them***..."*

Can you see with me that the scriptures reveal that there are greater experiences than water baptism; greater immersions from out of the spirit-realm than what our religious traditions and doctrines allowed us to believe!

Listen there is more available to us than what the ordinary religious fellow was made to believe!

"Then they laid their hands upon them, **and they received** *the Holy Spirit,"* it says in verse 17.

I don't want you to misunderstand me. I don't want you to look at the immersion of the Spirit as a separate added event or experience that you are somehow lacking and have to now go and pursue to add to salvation, no, **you have everything already inside of you; your spirit already has access to that unseen realm of the spirit and to the Holy Spirit Himself.**

Romans 5:2 makes it clear that, *"Through Him (through what was accomplished by Father God Himself in the person of Jesus Christ, **we have all obtained access by faith into His grace in which we already stand**..."*

The Holy Spirit and the things of the Spirit, including the language of the Spirit, or speaking in other tongues **is our inheritance, it is our right and privilege to access these things and live our lives In that dimension of the supernatural; that dimension of power.**

I say again: **The Holy Spirit and all His gifts is our portion already.**

Acts 2:39, *"This gift is for you and for your children and even for those who think themselves far off, it belongs to everyone who hears God's call to them in the gospel."*

It is just that many have not yet broken through in their spirit into that supernatural dimension of living, and come into this experience on their own, and that is where the laying on of hands come in, to assist someone else and impart and release the initial spark within their spirit that awakens them to that spirit-dimension that is already within them and helps to ignite them.

As they yield to that experience it leads to a full immersion in the Holy Spirit and a saturation of their spirit-being with the very love and presence of God to where the joy and oneness they experience in Him has to find expression and gushes forth from their inner-being in the language of the Spirit and in prophecy, praising and glorifying God. **It is like rivers of living water being released and gushing forth out of their inner-most being.**

You see; Jesus came and gave us a whole new perspective on these things! *He changed everything when it comes to our understanding of the supernatural dimension of the Spirit!*

Jesus came and changed everything when He revealed the startling truth that the kingdom of God is **within us**; that God doesn't live in temples made by human hands, but that God intended all along for Mankind to be His dwelling place, and **that we are the very temples of the Holy Spirit, and that the place God exists, the kingdom and domain of God in other words, *is therefore within us already,*** and not in outer space somewhere!

That truly changes everything!

Jesus revealed that what was lacking in Man was not access to the Holy Spirit, *but only the awareness of His nearness.*

He wants us to live our lives in the awareness that God's Spirit is the very Life of every person that comes into the world, and that our lives was only meant *to be lived in intimate relationship with Him,* and not in any other way.

You may think you have a human spirit apart from God, but *life was meant to be lived in union with God's Spirit,* not apart from Him.

There really is only one eternal Spirit *who gives life to every human spirit,* and there is no existence apart from Him.

"In Him we live and move and have our being. He gives to all Men, life, breath, and all other things!" - Acts 17:24-25, 28.

God is our very Life, our true essence, our very identity. That is why Jesus said that we need to lose our life in order that we might find it. The identity we hold ourselves to be (generated by our own thinking reasoning mind;) **that natural life identity we cling to is not who we really are.**

Listen; eternal life is not some afterlife gift, it is that amen, but it is first of all **the awareness within of the eternal Divine Presence**. He is called the Holy Spirit. It's all about knowing Him *intimately* - **an intimate relationship with our Maker - with Jesus; with Father God, in**

the Spirit, and therefore in spirit-dimension!
(John 17:3; 1 John 2:25; 1 John 5:20)

All that is necessary is not another added step, yet another *'Blessing,'* no, **all that is necessary is that *we come to the realization of that same Oneness which Jesus intimately knew within himself;* it's our legal right, our inheritance, our portion!**

Chapter 5

Speaking In The Spirit

Now let me emphasize this: In every other reference in the book of Acts where we are taught about people receiving that immersion in the Holy Spirit, immediately there was evidence of it, and people saw that evidence. All the scripture references talk about the new utterance that was given them by the Holy Spirit. They were speaking in other tongues and prophesying, glorifying God with great joy.

We are going to look at another one of those references in a little while in Acts chapter 10. Those people, as they received and embraced that immersion happening in their spirits, a new utterance was given them; they began to speak in the language of the Spirit.

Paul teaches us about that language of the Spirit, and also about its public use in a meeting setting in 1 Corinthians 14. Everyone usually focuses on the public use side of Paul's conversation with the Corinthians about this gift of other tongues, (or speaking the language of the Spirit,) **but he also said some very profound things about the importance of speaking in the language of the Spirit** and I want to highlight that for you in this book for just a second before we get into the other part of that conversation.

Paul says in verse 2 of 1 Corinthians 14: *"For one who speaks in that language of the Spirit speaks not to men but directly to God; for no one understand what that person is saying, because they are uttering mysteries in the spirit to God."*

Now that sounds important; speaking in the language of the Spirit sounds important, it does not sound insignificant and of no value to me. I believe it is of great value, even to us today still!

Paul also says in verse 14, *"For if I pray in other tongues* (in the language of the Spirit)*, **my spirit prays,** but my mind is disconnected or unfruitful* (It does not contribute to what is happening)*."*

In other words this is not a soul-realm thing; **this is a spirit-realm thing.**

Actually it is also interesting to note that there are two words in the original Greek used for the word *"other."*

The one is the word *"heteros"* meaning another of a different kind, like two books, but the one is a cook book written in English, and the other is a world history book written in French. They are both books, but books of a different kind. This word *"heteros"* is used when talking about speaking in other tongues. It is still a language, but it is unlike any other language spoken here on earth; **it is not an earthly language but a spiritual language, it's a language of another dimension, it's the language of the Spirit. It's a heavenly language** as opposed to an earthly language.

The other word used in the Greek is the word, *"allos."* meaning another of the same kind, like two Bibles, one may be in English and the other in French, but they are both Bibles. All the languages of the earth, even though they may be different, are all still earthly languages, thus I may speak Afrikaans and you may speak English. It is still another language but in the Greek the word *"allos"* would be used, because it's another language of the same kind.

So Paul says In 1 Corinthians 14:2,

*"For one who speaks in that language of the Spirit speaks not to men but **directly to God;** for no one understands what that person is saying, because **they are uttering mysteries in the spirit to God**."*

Verse 14, *"For if I pray in other tongues* (in the language of the Spirit)*, **my spirit prays**, but my mind is disconnected or unfruitful* (It does not contribute to what is happening)*."*

That is why in verse 13 he says that, *"...he who speaks in this unknown language of the Spirit (in other tongues) should trust in the Holy Spirit's enablement to interpret what is being said."*

57

He says in verse 5, *"Now I desire **all of you** to speak in other tongues; (in the language of the Spirit,) **so that** (or in order to) **that you may also be able to prophesy**."*

He actually confirms this in verse 18 by saying, *"I thank my God that I speak in other tongues, (in that language of the Spirit) **more than you all combined**..."*

In verse 15 he reveals why. He says: *"What is my goal with all this? I will pray with the spirit, **that I may pray with the mind also**; I will sing with the spirit **that I may sing with the mind also**."*

That is why he ends of in verse 39 with, *"So, my brethren, in conclusion, earnestly desire to prophecy, and therefore I tell you, **do not forbid speaking in other tongues**, (or the language of the Spirit)."*

So therefore **it is vital for us to grasp that praying in the spirit *precedes a new realm of understanding.***

You see, before I received that immersion in the Holy Spirit the scriptures talk about, I would as a young new very immature Christian pray with my understanding, and I would pray and relate to God my problem; how big it is and how long I've had it. But when I received the indwelling of the Holy Spirit and became immersed in that supernatural realm of the Spirit everything in my prayer-life changed. Now I was praying in the language of the Spirit and as I was praying in the spirit I was able to utter mysteries in the spirit-realm that my own mind could not at first understand, **but as I continued to pray in the language of the Spirit I was no longer bound to immature understanding,** *those mysteries began to unfold to my understanding;* **the Scriptures became alive with new interpretation, and fresh revelation from the Holy Spirit.** It is for instance out that realm of the Spirit, opened up to me by the Holy Spirit, that I was enabled by Him to write all these books, you see. They were all given birth to out of that supernatural realm of the Spirit.

So as you are praying in the language of the Spirit; as you are praying in the spirit and you make it your practice, your habit, and you continue in it, **you no longer merely understand like a child, but revelation begins to unfold to you** *and you begin to know what you are praying about,* **and you know where to look in the Scriptures and you know what God is trying to say to you and to others.**

Many have limited speaking in other tongues to something foolish that has no value; to just making a big noise, but I truly do believe the Scriptures reveal that **it is one of the most important gifts you can ever receive from the Holy Spirit.** *It opens the whole spirit-realm up to you and all the other gifts of the Spirit.*

I believe that that is exactly why Paul said in 1 Corinthians 14:18, *"I thank my God that I speak in other tongues, (in that language of the Spirit)* **more than you all combined.***"* And he was even addressing a group of zealous believers at that time that was idolizing that gift and speaking quite a bit more than other believers in other tongues. They were actually abusing the use of that gift and ability, because they didn't understand its proper use and significance, which was the reason Paul felt compelled to write to them with some well needed instruction, and yet Paul said: *"I speak in other tongues more than you all combined"* Ha... ha... ha...!

Speaking in other tongues was therefore very important to Paul!

Have you ever considered that it was *the very first gift* given to the apostles on the Day of Pentecost at their infilling of the Holy Spirit *because it was the most important gift?*

It was not the first gift given to them because it was the most insignificant and the least of the gifts, no, it was the first gift given to them, because it was the greatest of the gifts. And why do I say that? Because **it is the key that unlocks all the rest of the things of the Spirit to us so we can grasp it and function in it?**

'Now wait a minute brother Rudi' someone might say. *'Didn't Paul Himself essentially say*

60

just that, that this gift is insignificant, in 1 Corinthians 14?'

No He did not! We will get into that discussion in a little while, but I do not want you to get distracted right now by what you think you know and understand. Most of us have been misinformed and not taught accurately about these things!

I believe that it is key for us to learn to pray in the spirit **often** *and make it a habit* **to continue in it so that revelation knowledge may follow and flow freely as the Holy Spirit begins to open up and interpret more and more truth to your spirit, while you are reading the Scriptures, while you are worshiping, and while you are praising Him just living your life, staying sensitive to Him with an open ear, ready to receive some interpretation, some revelation that will quicken your spirit to that supernatural spirit-dimension and keep you refreshed and ignited with passion, full of His love and full of the Spirit.**

I recently heard some young smarty-pants whipper-snapper quote 1 Corinthians 13:8 saying that there is no need for the gifts of the Spirit anymore and that Paul himself said that tongues and prophecy will cease and that we have no need for it, and that only love will remain, because only love is important. He forgets that Paul in that same verse also said that knowledge will cease... ha... ha... ha...

Listen knowledge will always have its place of importance; where would we be if we didn't know and understand the gospel? Where would we be in any other arena even in this natural world we live in without proper knowledge or understanding of things? And in the same breath I might add that as long as we are in this world tongues and prophecy also has its place of importance.

Don't misunderstand me now; the Holy Spirit most certainly wants us to mature spiritually to the point where everything else fades in significance, in comparison with love.

But make no mistake, all the gifts of the Spirit matter to the Holy Spirit and He will continue to employ them all and challenge us to yield to Him and function in those gifts in order to help bring us all to a place of grasping the love of God and maturing in that love.

Maybe one day when we all reach the pinnacle of revelation and we are all mature in the things of the Spirit, and in the love of God, we will no longer need tongues or prophecy or any such things in our lives, **but as long as there are still new believers, and as long as immaturity remains and there is still a need for some growth and development in people these things will have their place of importance and cannot be done away with.**

The truth is; as long as there still is such a thing as a natural existence, you know, real people living in a real world with some very real needs, *there will continue to be a need for the gifts of the Spirit, and both speaking in other tongues, and prophecy, will have its place.*

The gifts of the Spirit is all part of God's love finding expression through us in this world, and therefore we cannot view the gifts of the Spirit as somehow a separate issue removed from love; as somehow outside of Love's expression of Himself in the earth today!

We will get back to Simon the magician eventually, I promise, ha... ha... ha...

I am just going into all this for the sake of you knew believers out there who have just recently come into this immersion experience into the supernatural dimension of the Holy Spirit yourselves, or you may not know about these things; this immersion of power in the Holy Spirit, or perhaps this is for you believers who have been miss-informed and taught against these things, or have been taught very little about it and are therefore unfamiliar with the things of the Spirit and the language of the Spirit.

Listen I am not writing these things to offend you, but to help you break out of the realm of your intellect and into the spirit-realm.

Trust me, that realm of the Spirit is way more dynamic than the soul-realm. I have been living the most exciting life, caught up in this realm of the Spirit for over 40 years now, and I wouldn't trade it for anything in the world!

Being immersed in the Holy Spirit is the most satisfying exciting life you can possibly live, and I can't emphasize that enough, it is exactly what Jesus was referring to when He talked about life more abundantly (John 10:10; John 7:37-39; Acts 1:5 and 1:8)

But let's quickly get into the other part of that teaching of Paul in 1 Corinthians 14 concerning the public use of the language of the Spirit; or the public speaking in other tongues in a meeting scenario or a social gathering scenario.

When Paul asks the question in 1 Corinthians 12:30, *"Do all speak in tongues?"* He was not saying that this gift of speaking in other tongues or the language of the Spirit is not for us all and that not all believers can receive that ability from the Holy Spirit. He was merely referring to a manifestation for the sake of ministry to others; he was referring to what we call: a message in tongues, *and not about that gift of being able to communicate with the Holy Spirit in the language of the Spirit, or in other tongues as it is also referred to.* Obviously not everyone has learned to function in that capacity of ministry, to be able to publicly give a supernatural message in other tongues to a congregation of believers, but some have, and really the rest of us can too as we mature in the things of the Holy Spirit, it's not off-limits to any of us, Paul was just making a specific point here. **That is why I brought that passage of scripture up,** *because I do not want you to hold to any reason in your mind to disqualify yourself from being able to learn how to flow and become comfortable with and adapt in the language of the Spirit, or speaking in other tongues*. **Religion has lied to us for way too long about these things, because they misinterpreted what was said, and didn't understand or function in these things themselves. Their ignorance is no reason for us to remain in ignorance ourselves. These things belong to us as sons and daughters of God and it's high time for us to learn to function in them.**

Now let's get back to 1 Corinthians 14. Paul says, not all can, and not all should speak forth a message in tongues to the *"church..."* (The *'ekklesia'* in the Greek – those who know and understand their spiritual identity as children of God, and therefore consider one another as brothers and sisters, part of the same family unit; the family of God)

What this scripture is trying to say is that when God wants to give a special message to a congregation or group of people, whether they are 2 or 3 or 300, God is *not* going to use 300 voices to give that special message to the congregation or group, *but He will move upon one person and inspire them and empower them to manifest that gift.*

And who will that person be? It can be anybody sensitive to the Holy Spirit and tuning in to the fact that He wants to say something important enough to interrupt the regular scheduled program. But It is usually the ones who have an intimate relationship with God and intimately knows the indwelling Holy Spirit and are already familiar with the language of the Spirit and knows how to yield to and flow with the Holy Spirit and bring forth that utterance in the Spirit.

This is different from all of us praying together or singing together in the language of the Spirit; we are talking about a message in the Spirit now, from God to Man.

When that utterance begins to come forth under the unction of the Holy Spirit, those who know the things of the Spirit can easily sense the difference in their spirit between that kind of message and just regular speaking in other tongues, and they immediately know that God is saying something supernaturally to this congregation, or group of people, and so they immediately ask God, quietly, there in their hearts, for the interpretation of what is being said, and once they know, then the interpretation follows the message and they begin to explain to the group what God is saying to that congregation. It is almost always something unexpected and Spirit-inspired and full of edification, exhortation and comfort; it is something no one prepared for in their preparations from the Word to bring a message to the group, it is something which the Holy Spirit just quickens within that person's heart in the spur of the moment.

It can come in many ways, so I am not saying that this is the way it always happens or is supposed to happen. We can't put the living person of the Holy Spirit in a box and expect Him to always act predictably. He has a way of always surprising us and braking out of the box in spontaneous unpredictable ways. That's why it's important to maintain a living relationship with a living Holy Spirit. He is the living God, amen.

Let's read 1 Corinthians 14:18 again, *"I thank my God that I speak in other tongues, (in that language of the Spirit)* **more than you all combined,**" but then he says in verse 19, *"nevertheless, in the "church,"* (in the congregation of the saints; in the gathering of a group) *I would rather speak 5 words with my mind in order to instruct others, than 10,000 words in other tongues."*

He says back in verse 5 & 6, *"Now, if I come to you speaking in the language of the Spirit; speaking in other tongues only, how shall that benefit you unless I bring some kind of message in tongues and interpretation of it, or I bring some revelation or knowledge or prophecy or some teaching and instruction?"*

Paul's greatest gift in the church was to teach, amen, and not to speak in tongues.

Paul fully recognized that teaching and instructing people was a more valuable gift in a group setting than speaking in tongues, **but he did not say that the language of the Spirit, or other tongues are without importance,** because he made it clear that it was very important to him when he said, *"I thank my God that I speak in other tongues, (in that language of the Spirit) more than you all combined."*

So, if he prayed in tongues so much, where did he pray? Where did he speak in tongues and pray in tongues more than them all? Certainly not in a congregational setting, but in his own private devotion of His heart, at home, or on the road, or wherever he went, amen.

Speaking or praying in other tongues; in that language of the Spirit was Paul's practice, it was his habit, amen, *and he passed it on to other believers, because he believed in its importance.* He knew that there was something to this gift, to this manifestation of the Spirit, to this language of the Spirit that was valuable to him; it added something to his spirit, amen, he knew it edified him, and he even wrote later on and encouraged the saints to *"pray at all times in the Spirit, to build yourselves up in your faith."*

Paul personally experienced the edification that came through speaking in other tongues, and praying in that language of the Spirit.

I was myself personally immersed in the Holy Spirit at 7 or 8 years of age, while I was still reading the book of acts one day and studying about the gifts of the Spirit *because I was hungry to know more about the subject.* God suddenly interrupted my studies with the supernatural and I found myself praying in other tongues, but the enemy played tricks in my mind because I didn't know better and I convinced myself that it was just me jabbering on and making this stuff all up, and so I reasoned it away and it stopped, and for almost the better part of that year no one taught me to use this gift, but thank God it happened again in a prayer meeting and my dad was there to witness it, and so my parents and my precious Grandma began to teach me about it and I grew and matured in the things of the Spirit. Thank God they knew and were taught about these things.

You see if you get a gift and you don't use it that gift becomes useless to you.

At one time in my life somebody actually gave me a car, a grayish little 4 door Honda Accord, and I was so thankful and praised God for it, and I sure didn't just let it sit there and get rusty and moldy, no, somebody taught me how to drive and *I used it.* I drove that thing into the ground... ha... ha... ha... It was a gift to be used; it was intended to be used, amen.

Praise God that you have been given a pair of hands, but if you don't learn how to use the hands you already have, those hands will become useless to you.

Listen, when God gives us the infilling in the Holy Spirit, and from out of that supernatural dimension gives us different manifestations of the Spirit, He expects us to use our spirit in those gifts, amen.

I thank God that I was taught on how to use and cultivate that gift of speaking in other tongues, and praying often in the language of the Spirit, and make it a habit to pray in the Spirit at all times, whether I go to bed or wake up, or whether I drive my bicycle or later my car or whatever I do. I learned to keep praying in the Spirit, speaking in other tongues, edifying my spirit, building my spirit up in strength **and eventually the whole supernatural dimension of the Holy Spirit opened up to me and I began to have access to all the gifts of the Spirit to use them in ministry to others.**

Just like we exercise our bodies to get our bodies to a better standard of fitness, it is necessary that we develop our spirit-man, **because there is a potential in your spirit that God wants to awaken and educate, so that He can release the supernatural through your life!**

Hey, if you have not been immersed in the Holy Spirit yet, you don't need to shut your ears and close this book now, thinking, *'Well, this is obviously not for me.'* No, you can be immersed in the spirit while you are still reading this book, before you put it down even.

If you don't speak in other tongues yet, **you can *receive* it right now,** you don't have to wait for anything, just ask Daddy God for the ability to speak in the Spirit right now, *and expect something to happen!* Begin to open yourself up to the presence of the Holy Spirit, become conscious of Him in your spirit, and aware of His nearness, *and then just begin to yield yourself; yield your spirit to the Holy Spirit **and open your mouth and begin to speak,*** allowing the Holy Spirit to give you utterance of that language of the Spirit, *and it will come forth and begin to flow as you yield more and more and **allow it to happen** to you.*

Acts 2:4 makes it clear: *"And they were all filled with the Holy Spirit* (they fully embraced that infilling)*, and **they began** to speak in other tongues as the Spirit gave **them** utterance of it."*

He didn't force their mouths open with a pry-bar. No, it says, *"**They** began to speak..."*

Acts 19:6 confirms this: *"And when Paul had laid his hands upon them, the Holy Spirit came on them; and **they spoke** with other tongues and prophesied."*

Acts 8:17 basically says the same thing, *"They laid their hands on them, and **they received (embraced)** the Holy Spirit."*

71

How did they know that they had received the Holy Spirit?

I want you to picture with me the whole scenario as it plays out here in this scripture.

Peter and John, 2 leaders from Jerusalem came and said, *'Listen guys, everything that Philip told you is true, and so we have come to confirm that word which he preached to you about Jesus Christ and about the kingdom of God, but we also want you to know that knowing these things is only the beginning of your experience in God, God wants to bring you into a deeper more intimate knowledge and experience of Him, of His person and of His Spirit and of His love and of His power. Yes, you heard us correctly; you too can know and experience the power of God, that same power that flows through Philip. Philip is one of the young guys a part of our ministry; he is just an ordinary young man like many of you, there is nothing more special to him than there is to you. That same power that you have seen in manifestation and can bear witness to in Philip's life, you can tap into that power as well; it is available and within easy reach to every one of you, because it was God's promise to us all through our mutual father, Abraham. Jesus came and He removed the curse of the Fall and of the Law; the curse of guilt and shame (Galatians 3:14) **so that we can possess the promised Holy Spirit.** Listen man, guilty feelings of shame can no* *longer separate us from the promise of God; from God's gift to us.'*

And so the scriptures go on to tell us what happened next, *"They laid their hands on them, **and they received** the Holy Spirit."*

You see the only thing that can possible separate any of us now and stop us from receiving is ignorance, and that is why Peter and John came to Samaria to deal with that ignorance and help the Samaritans fully open up to that supernatural dimension and receive the things of the Holy Spirit.

But let me tell you something; the worst kind of ignorance in the world is willful ignorance. Willful ignorance is when you refuse to embrace and accept and yield to what you have heard, and you choose rather to ignore what you have heard and understood and now know. That kind of ignorance is inexcusable and unacceptable! The Holy Spirit cannot manifest where ignorance prevails. This is why Paul also then begins his teaching on the gifts of the Spirit in 1 Corinthians 12:1 with, *"Concerning Spiritual things brethren, I do not want you to be ignorant!"*

Listen man, ignorance is a thief, and it will rob God's *"church"* of the supernatural and it will also rob you as an individual of the supernatural, and so you'll find yourself and you'll just have to settle for the ordinary, ***but I*** *am here to tell you that you don't need to, amen!*

It is not necessary for even just one Christian to lack the supernatural in their life!

I really believe that from the youngest to the oldest we may all receive that immersion in the Holy Spirit and His power, and witness an increase of the supernatural and the miraculous manifesting in our lives, on a daily basis!

Chapter 6

Simon's Folly

Acts 8:17, *"Peter and John laid their hands on them, **and they <u>received</u>** the Holy Spirit."*

Now in this particular instance here it does not say to us that they spoke in other tongues or prophesied, but it is quite obvious that something supernatural must have happened; something out of the ordinary must have manifested.

Why do I say that?

Because in verse 13 it says that Simon the sorcerer also believed and he was amazed when he saw great signs and miracles performed in front of his eyes. So obviously he saw some things before, he saw the healings, he saw the miracles performed by Philip, *but when it comes to the immersion in the Holy Spirit, he has never seen anything like this before, nothing as powerful and life-changing.*

He saw many things in Philip's life and ministry that amazed him, but here all of a sudden something more intriguing takes place, suddenly Simon sees that these men, they look like ordinary men, just like Philip, they are not all dressed up in religious apparel, but there is something supernatural and even more intriguing to Simon happening through their ministry.

Just as a side note: I do not believe that it is necessary to get all wrapped up in religious apparel, as long as a person's heart is clothed with the garments of righteousness; the preciousness of the robe of righteousness. It's our awareness of the spirit-righteousness we are already clothed with that makes us holy; that separates us from the ordinary and takes away our nakedness and shame and prepares us for ministry to others.

So here are these *'ordinary men'* as far as Simon is concerned, laying their hands on some other ordinary people, some ordinary believers. I mean, Simon knew many of those ordinary Samaritan believers, after all they once followed him and praised him as *'The Great Power of God,'* but something happened to them and now they are so different, it is like they got transformed in just a short little while, and with some of them it was almost immediately, and the difference was like night and day, and now here they suddenly began to do something that he has never seen.

I believe he saw them spoke in other tongues as well as prophecy, because Simon wouldn't offer Peter and John money to be able to do the same things Peter and John did if he saw nothing.

Look at it again there in verse 18 & 19 of Acts 8, *"Now when Simon saw that the Holy Spirit was given through the laying on of the apostle's hands, he offered them money, saying, 'Give me also this power, that anyone on whom I lay hands may receive the Holy Spirit.'"*

Do you really think that if Simon saw nothing he would have offered them money? No he wouldn't have. But what did he see? He saw a power released, he saw the supernatural, he heard the language of the Spirit come out of these ordinary people's mouths, and he saw them in absolute ecstasy and in total joy prophetically glorifying God and saying very profound prophetic things he has never heard before but which his spirit-man instinctively knew were true. He saw such an outpouring of love towards God and other people as he has never seen before, amen! **He saw the very evidence of the glory of God coming upon those people!**

And so he says, verse 19, *"Give me also this power, that anyone whom I lay my hands upon may receive this Holy Spirit."*

But Peter knew that the motives of his heart weren't right. The Holy Spirit inside of Peter saw right through Simon and exposed his selfish motives so that he can get free from them before he could go any further with God in the things of the Spirit, otherwise he would abuse it and end up hurting other people and bring shame on the name of Jesus.

Let this be a warning to us also in ministry!

The Holy Spirit wasn't going to permit him in his hidden selfish motives to continue to try and manipulate and deceive and abuse people, all for his own agenda of greed and fame.

I thank God that Peter had enough of a discerning spirit, and he had enough love in his heart for Simon to tell him the truth and hopefully help him get free from that rotten, festering condition in his soul.

Peter sure didn't speak to him in a very encouraging way, and in some cases that might be very necessary and helpful, even today still, regardless of how some may feel and what some may think about it in our supposed more enlightened society.

Verse 20 says, *"But Peter said to him, 'You are perishing with your silver, because you are warped in your thinking. How is it that you thought you could obtain **the gift** of God with money?"*

Simon, don't you see that if somebody brought you a **gift**, and you now want to pay for that **gift**, *you insult the giver!* It could only be because you don't believe you deserve it. Is it perhaps that there are hidden motives in your heart you feel guilty about and are ashamed of?

Can you see how religion was prepared to pay any price for the supernatural! Even today still, they are prepared to pay any price, to do anything; to fast, to pray, to read their Bible, to go to church faithfully every time the doors open, to labor for God and the pastor. They will do just about anything for the supernatural, but even after all their prayer and fasting, and after all their labor *they still end up with nothing,* because instead of fully embracing the truth of the gospel and falling in love with Father God and with others, their hearts are full of compromise and corruption! They don't really believe and trust and love God nearly as much as they love themselves!

Simon, you cannot earn the supernatural! You cannot buy the gift of God! I can sense that because you are trying to buy the gift of God, there is obviously something else going on in your heart; something else at work in your spirit. In fact I sense someone else at work here Simon; you need to stop letting the devil have his way with you! Stop yielding to him and stop lying to yourself about your hidden motives and agenda! All it takes is a pure heart Simon! All it takes is yielding to the love of God and receiving from the heart Simon! All it takes is faith, Simon, genuine faith, not something fake, not playing games and pretending. Because Simon, I can see that instead of falling in love with God, you are still pursuing fame and fortune. **Open yourself up to really hear the truth of the gospel first, Simon, and as you open yourself up to the love of God revealed in that gospel, to truly receive and embrace that love and make room for it in your heart, the gospel itself, that very love of God will transform you and give you a pure heart, and that's all it takes!**

Verse 21, *"But as for now you have neither part nor lot in this matter, for your heart is not right before God! Therefore repent immediately of this wickedness of yours, and look to the Lord to wash you in His forgiveness and love and set you completely free from the whacked-out intentions of your heart, because it is indeed possible to be free brother!"*

You see, even after all that he saw and was a part of, he was still not partaking of it for himself in his own heart, just like Judas Iscariot and many others.

Peter arrested Simon in his spirit with that sharp loving rebuke and Simon came under conviction in his heart, knowing that it was all true, and that he can't play games with God anymore, and so he immediately begged Peter, verse 24, *"Pray for me to the Lord, right here and now please, that nothing of what you said may come upon me, I don't want to be ruled by greed! I don't want to perish with my money, like a mere man with his silver, I want a better life than that; a better life than living for*

money and being ruled by money and a
misguided desire for fame and recognition!"

But I want you to notice also that Peter didn't just do that; he didn't pray for Simon right away and then lay hands on him to be filled with the Spirit also. No, he left Simon to sort things out in his own heart between himself and God. Sometimes people need to be left alone with that hell of their own making, disqualifying themselves, **until they have faced their own hearts before God, not considering their own sin so much as *considering the enormity of His love for them,* and thus confronting themselves and their sin with the truth of the gospel, so that they can come to some strong faith-conclusions from the heart, and come to a place of no longer disqualifying themselves from that glorious thing God intended for them all along and wants to bring them fully into.**

Let me say it again: Religion was and is prepared to pay any price for the supernatural. Religion is prepared to do anything - to fast, to pray, to labor, to do anything for the supernatural, but here comes Paul and he spoils it all in Galatians Chapter Three. He says in Galatians 3:2 and again in verse 5, *"Did you receive the Spirit, and does God do miracles among you through the hearing of faith, or through your labor in the law; your diligence in religion - in obeying religious regulations? No, he says, come on man, we received when we heard, and what we heard* *brought forth a faith within us which purified our hearts impacting us with the love of God, and we grasped what God desired to do amongst us, and because of that faith impact, that love impact **we receive**!"*

He goes on to say, *"Now don't go and try and complete in the flesh **what began in the spirit.**"*

It's that gospel truth we fully embrace which so mightily works within us now, hallelujah!

It's His Word abiding in us which bears its own fruit!

You see we have so often thought that we could go and patch up that old religious system; those old beliefs, that old worn out garment, and patch it through fasting and through praying and through trying in our own efforts to try and get our own hearts right and get right with God again, and straighten things out between us and Him, and get favor with God again.

But it doesn't work that way, amen, it never really works, and if it does it is short lived, and then we have to start the process all over again, and we find ourselves trapped under the Old Covenant; under that old outdated system again!

E.W. Kenyon wrote in one of his books called: Two Kinds Of Righteousness, he says we'll pay any price for righteousness, we'll go through any amount of sacrifice and restitution and repentance and confessing of our sins, but all we end up with is not the righteousness of God, but *the righteousness of works; **a righteousness of our own making,** **instead of the righteousness of Jesus Christ!***

That righteousness can only be embraced through faith!

You see the religious world built up all kinds of doctrines so that through the merits of those performances under those doctrines we could qualify to receive from God. But it's not the truth! They have lied to us! According to the New Testament **we already qualify, every person already qualify to receive from God,** because of God's own performance in the person of Jesus Christ; because of Jesus Christ's performance, amen, not ours!

The gospel of the New Testament is built upon Him, amen; it's built upon the Son of God who prevailed mightily in the flesh, and in the cross, and through the resurrection, on our behalf. In that resurrection we were raised; we were elevated to a new position. We are accepted in the Beloved; we are seated with Jesus in the very bosom of the Father! That resurrection was our resurrection; it was our victory, through Jesus Christ, amen!

Now before you get mad at me let me just add this: There is still a place for fasting and for prayer, even now, in New Testament times, but it's a different kind of fasting, it's a different kind of prayer. In the Old Covenant times Man had a certain kind of approach to God, it was an approach under the Law and through the Law, but now in the New Testament times we have a new unreserved approach. We can come boldly before our Father, amen; we can come boldly to the throne of grace **that we might receive** in times of need! Hallelujah!

Now with confidence we may come in through that torn veil, the veil of His flesh, amen!

Jesus died, actually God the Father came in person, and He died in Jesus, demonstrating His love in the clearest possible way, *so that we can be reconciled to Him and come to Him with confidence!*

And now in that light we read about the apostles fasting over there in Acts 13 and it says, *"They were ministering unto the Lord and fasting..."*

Can you see that their fast was now motivated by love, by a desire to spend time with the God of love, who is in love with them, and minister unto Him with the kisses of their mouth, the offerings from their lips, singing love songs and praises unto Him, loving on Jesus with whom they are head over heels in love with, because they are already righteous through His doing and not their own, and they were celebrating that, instead of still trying to become righteous

84

and obtain righteousness on their own. Their prayer and fasting was motivated by love and faith, and not by need. There's a difference, a big difference, amen!

When we now pray, we pray **from** the throne room, seated in Christ in heavenly places. We pray from that direction, from a place of strength and confidence, **conscious of our oneness with Him, conscious of this love-affair He initiated, conscious of this mighty love we are cherishing and enjoying here in our hearts, in our bosom's, between us and the living Holy Spirit of God.**

Conscious of that love within us; conscious of His love for us, our faith now works and it functions and it accomplishes much, amen!

So the secret is: Hearing with faith; not our religious labors and efforts! Faith works by love, amen, and we have a different authority, and we have a different attitude in our prayers and our intersession!

Alright, now where were we before I got all distracted? Ha... ha... ha...

Okay, in contrast to Simon we have Philip and I want us to go back and quickly look at this young man Philip and discover his purity of heart and what made him such a dynamic guy with such a powerful influence. He totally impacted the whole city of Samaria. Let me just give you a little background first before we get into the text.

Chapter 7

Philip The Deacon/Evangelist

Here in Acts 8 you have Philip preaching the good news in Samaria. He was just a little deacon, but I praise God that the Holy Spirit in us doesn't just settle for deacons, for just ordinary men with man-made titles, and neither should we, amen!

You can go read there in Acts chapter 6 for yourself how Philip was one of those seven guys that was appointed to a certain office in the church in Jerusalem; they had a specific function, while the big shot apostles went and they prayed and they were in the Scriptures studying the Word and they preached and they ministered to people. But here you have this ordinary guy who entered into an extra ordinary ministry. He preached the good news about the name of Jesus Christ, and about the kingdom of God being within us and within our reach, in Samaria, to the here to shunned Samaritans. Those people believed and they were immersed, both men and women, into Jesus Christ and what He represents.

You see Philip was fulfilling Acts 1:8. Jesus said: *"You shall receive power when the Holy Spirit comes and overwhelms you from within, and you shall be My witnesses in Jerusalem, but it will not stay there, in Judea and Samaria also, but even to the utter most parts of the earth you will be My witnesses."*

Now as I already said before, it was contrary to the Jewish mind, especially in the light of the political sentiment of their day, as well as their religious feelings of bigotry, to even consider bringing witness to the Samaritans, because they had no dealings with Samaritans. But Jesus included Samaria in the gospel. Praise God! He included every tribe, every tongue, and every nation in the good news to be proclaimed.

And so here you have this young man, Philip, he didn't even go through their Bible School, he wasn't even fully ordained, he didn't even have a proper title in their organization, just a simple function as a deacon, one of the lowest titles you could possibly have. It was his job to watch the tables during meal times and serve people sitting at those tables, so he was basically a waiter and a busboy, but inside of his spirit he knew that his ministry to people was not limited to just some small function behind a table. This young man understood that there was a tremendous anointing and authority available to him, that he could walk in, to the same measure as Peter and John and the other apostles walked in it. He grasped that the ministry of the Holy Spirit was not limited to a guy standing behind the pulpit, or to just a select few. But within his spirit he knew that he can just be an ordinary fellow in the congregation **and continue to love on people without loosing anything in God.**

You see he had come to such a place in God where titles didn't matter at all; *he had come to such a faith relationship with God in the truth of the gospel,* **such an intimate relationship, a love-affair with God,** that the very dimension of the Spirit, the supernatural extra ordinary dimension of Spirit-power *began to flow freely through his spirit.*

And so the Scriptures say that he went to Samaria. And he didn't even ask for their approval, you know, the apostolic counsel in the church in Jerusalem, he didn't feel the need to ask their permission, he just went with a heart full of love, burning with a desire to include the Samaritans in proclaiming the good news to them also.

You see he did something new no one else up to that point had done or even tried to do. He went into an area where the ordinary Jew wouldn't go, where the apostles wouldn't even go, and so he went into Samaria and he preached the gospel, and began to proclaim and reveal to them the Christ.

I'm so glad that Philip didn't go into Samaria and try with some plausible words to get a crowd together and try and persuade them with cleverly devised man-made philosophies and confusing little religious arguments.

Now I want you to know that the ministry strategy we read about in Acts is still the New Testament strategy, it is still God's strategy for us, for now, for this hour. Hallelujah!

Listen Acts 8:6 says that when the crowds heard Philip's message and saw the signs he performed, multitudes with one accord gave heed to what was said by Philip; they all paid close attention to his message, for, it says in verse 7, *"With shrieks impure spirits came out of people, and many who were suffering in their joints and had problems with their limbs because of pain, whether they be paralyzed or lame, were healed. And so there was great joy in that city!"*

Unclean spirits can be loud sometimes, but we have much greater reason to be loud, hallelujah! Ha... ha... ha...

Isaiah 40:9 says, *"Get yourself up to a high mountain."* That means, don't go and hide your testimony in the valleys of life somewhere, no, *"Get yourself up to a high mountain,"* and then lift up your voice in a whisper? No! Ha... ha... ha... It says, *"Lift up your voice with strength, o herald of good tidings!"*

I want us to pay attention and take notice that there was definitely something happening there in Samaria, the whole city was abuzz with what was taking place. Philip was loud about the gospel, and the effects of the gospel were disturbing too. It wasn't a neat little quiet affair happening in some dark alley somewhere out of sight and out of mind. That's what the enemies of the gospel would have liked I'm sure. They would love for us to just keep things at a whisper, calm and collected. No! It's about time somebody gets excited about the gospel!

Hey listen we need to get used to some noise. I know it might disturb the frame of mind of some of you, but the Scriptures reveal that in heaven, in that unseen realm of spirit-reality where God and His angels exist together with all those who love Him, there is a constant thunder not caused by the elements, but caused by the spirits of just men made perfect, who praise God and explode in exaltation of the King. Their worship of Him is like the sound of many waters; like the sound of the abundance of rain even.

See no one even knew about this fellow, Philip, he wasn't one of the big names, but through the gospel there was something happening between Him and God, something deep and intimate, something real and wonderful, and he came and he preached in Samaria and he shook up all of Samaria.

Obviously the secret to that kind of impact wasn't in his fame or notoriety, no, there was something supernatural, something extra ordinary that accompanied his words; that accompanied the truth and good news of the gospel he was proclaiming with such boldness and confidence, and the content of those words brought conviction to multitudes of people.

Now it's alright to persuade one or two because of your time that you spend with them and out-argue them and win them over, but when you want to have multitudes respond to the gospel, then there needs to be the evidence of the supernatural, of the extra ordinary; the signs and wonders that accompany the truth of the gospel, to bring conviction and persuasion, to cut through those layers of tradition and warped religious thinking and those indifferent minds that says that, *'We don't believe in the supernatural; we don't believe in the love of God, we don't even believe there is a God. This stuff is not for our day, we don't believe, we are educated scientific people after all, and we are content to settle for the natural, for an ordinary existence, that is what is normal to us'*

But hey listen, God says, do not settle for what may be normal, you'll die, like mere men; do not settle for just an ordinary natural existence, because you are not just mere men subject to everything that comes your way in the natural! God wants the extra ordinary to accompany the life of the believer.

Listen; God wants the nearness, the very presence of the Holy Spirit to overshadow you so that Psalm 91 is not just another nice little bumper sticker to you. Praise God that was a nice idea to put it on your car as a bumper sticker, but it's not just a little reference that I vaguely relate to from time to time, but I live under the shadow of the Most High, amen! It's my dwelling place! There is evidence of His love in my heart! There's evidence of His presence in my life! And that evidence introduces the supernatural in my life!

That city of Samaria responded with great joy, because the good news became evident to the people; it became practical news.

They realized that this good news message was not just a pie in the sky message about maybe inheriting Heaven one day, no; they understood that it is news that affect my daily life right now. It is news that takes an ordinary man and transform that ordinary man into someone extra ordinary, amen, *because the impossible God now links up with me, He links up with me; that God of the impossible to whom nothing is impossible, He links up with me **and He lifts me up,** so I can mount up and fly with new wings on the winds of the Spirit, just like eagles do!*

Praise God that city did not respond with indifference, they didn't respond with unbelief and arguments, but they responded with great joy, because of the impact Philip and his message made upon them!

They heard and they saw! And something extra ordinary, something supernatural began to happen to them: *They began to truly hear and truly see,* **because there was an interruption in the natural by the supernatural.**

I am emphasizing these things to you, because I am confident and know that the Holy Spirit is building up inside of your spirit a faith to receive what I am saying. He is building up inside of your spirit a platform to operate from and know that you are going to see God in action in your own life, not just some vague future hope of Him possibly doing something through you, but you know that you will see God acting on your behalf *in the now,* demonstrating His power to you and through you on behalf of your community and on behalf of your country and on behalf of the other nations of this world and that generation you represent.

Listen I can't emphasize enough that God desires to manifest His glory. He is not a secret God that does things in secret service, off in a corner somewhere where no one takes note. God doesn't do anything in secret that He does not intend to be heralded from the rooftops. **He desires to manifest His love and His glory for all to see, that none may perish but all may come to a saving knowledge of the truth.**

God has something to say to the nations and I believe we are going to see God convince the nations again in our day of His reality, and of the truth of the gospel, of the reality of His love, through ordinary people so saturated by His love and truth that they become those extra ordinary heroes the world is waiting on. All of creation is groaning today still for the manifestation in our day of the sons of God!

But you see so often in our approach to the gospel and to God we so compromise with religion and with the world around us, so scared that we may step on some toes; that we might offend their way of thinking, that we shut up instead of speaking up.

There is a noise concerning the love of God, concerning the beauty and power of the grace of God that I am hearing in my spirit and that I am convinced we will soon hear and see in its effect, even to the utter most parts of the earth!

I have news for you who read this book and dare to read some of my other books as well, and begin to understand the full content of the gospel of grace: **Your voice is part of that noise!** Your voice is part of the volume of that sound in the earth today. Your voice is not going to be limited to some church meeting on a Sunday morning, to just some small sphere of influence, *but your voice is going to proclaim the glory of the kingdom of God within every person and within everyone's reach.* You are going to begin to proclaim loudly the name of Jesus, and as you begin to do that you are going to begin to witness signs and wonders happening through your life. And as you see that, you are going to begin to get a boldness you have never had before!

I remember when I was just a young man, 18 at the time, a friend and I when out witnessing together and we got to a little neighborhood gas station and there Alistair and I engaged another young man about our age in a conversation about Jesus, but the young man was full of new age philosophy and believed in reincarnation, so Alistair had difficulty explaining the true gospel to this guy, I mean the guy didn't really have ears to hear, he was very argumentative and opinionated, and suddenly Alistair interrupted him and blurted out, *'Man you do have quite an ugly devil inside of you, don't you?!'* and then Alistair simply proceeded to take authority over that spirit of confusion and command it to come out of the guy in Jesus name. And to my amazement the guy immediately began to cry and totally changed his whole demeanor and within 5 minutes it was clear that he had totally embraced Jesus and the truth of the gospel in his heart. Wow, I will never forget that supernatural experience with Alistair Trout that day as long as I live! And I can tell you story after story of supernatural experiences just like that one, but I don't have the time to get into all of that right now... ha... ha.... ha...!

Listen; we really need to learn to lean hard not upon our own understanding, but trust fully in the Holy Spirit and His guidance in our every conversation with people about the gospel. I say again: We must not lean so much upon our cleaver minds and our way of thinking, and our little 5 points of approach or whatever. Praise God for those things, but there's a better way, amen! Let's allow the Holy Spirit to lead and do His kind of outreach, His kind of conviction through our lives, the supernatural kind that brings about real reconciliation, and makes someone genuinely fall in love with Father God, amen!

Praise God, so, there was much joy in that city of Samaria. Can you begin to imagine that for your town, can you see your neighborhood rejoicing over the gospel?

I can just see some of you with your little group of friends already going to your local grocery store and getting all exited in conversation over the gospel, even running with the carts down the aisles, and the whole place exploding in joy and laughter and loud praised unto God, because everyone has a vibrant relationship with God and everyone has a testimony, somebody even telling of how their aunt or uncle was healed of cancer. And I can see one of the onlookers getting touched by God and healed as well as they listen and get sucked in by the vortex of your joy and swept up in your testimony!

Don't be a doubting Thomas now, I can see it already... ha... ha... ha...!

There will be testimony upon testimony upon testimony that will put the devil, or any other adversary of faith, to public shame, amen!

I lifted up my voice in a public place to a crowd of people in front of a grocery store during a busy holiday not so long ago, and I said to the people: *'Many of you may be offended because I am lifting up my voice in public, but Jesus hung in public just to convince you of how much He loves you, of how much you are worth to Father God. Listen, Jesus took our shame upon Himself, He hung naked in public, He was bare and vulnerable before all humanity, He made himself vulnerable and laid His heart bare, He did it publicly before the eyes of those who mocked and scorned, just so He could release us from the guilt and shame that covered us and ruled us. Many people think that they have need of nothing, but they do not know that they are pitiably, that they are poor, and they are wretched, they are naked, but I've got a message for you, God says: 'I counsel you today, come back to Me and receive from Me love and joy and fulfillment in abundance!'*

Something supernatural started to happen, I could sense it in my spirit, it was almost tangible in the atmosphere, and some of those people started silently weeping and came to me afterwards asking for prayer.

I still remember this one lady, sobbing uncontrollably, saying that she had prayed that, if there even is a God and if He really cares about her, to give her a sign that He loves her, or she couldn't go on anymore, and I had the privilege of sharing with her the lengths her Daddy God went to in Christ to demonstrate His love for her and reconcile her to Himself. Then I laid hands on her and she got filled with the Holy Spirit right there and then, and she never even heard of such things before.

I really do believe that the true gospel of God is going to be grasped and clearly made known again in our generation, and I am not talking about the watered down confusing man-made religious version of it we have heard for way to long, but the true gospel of God is going to be made known, and there is going to be such an outbreak of joy in many places around the globe, because many are going to have a testimony of what happened to their aunt, to their mom and dad, or to their brother or sister, they will all have a a testimony and there will be great joy generated globally, through the evidence of the supernatural, because the Holy Spirit is allowed to have His way because we are all finally beginning to rightly discern the Word of truth; the gospel of our reconciliation and salvation!

Listen I am telling you, the Bible is not just a book playing games with us, full of man-made philosophies, written by men to manipulate us religiously. This Word, this gospel of God that is woven like a golden thread into the very fabric of the whole Bible, hidden within the

Scriptures of old, and made known in the New Testament portion, is not just a fairytale, it's not just some nice but confusing little religious essay, but it has become to us and many others **the truth,** and as we read it and study it and meditate upon it, **we become consumed with it,** and so it has to us, and will soon become again in the whole world, **a constraining influence** to masses of people, and they will be feeling and saying just like us,

'God, Your Word is of integrity, and it promises that signs and wonders will follow those who believe, and I want You to know that I am not a doubter God, I am a believer, I believe Your Word, I have become persuaded in the truth of the gospel and of Your love for me and all other people and of Your person and of Your power God.'

'God, I believe in You, I believe the gospel above every other evidence, I believe it above the evidence of my own mind; that evidence my mind tries to produce contrary to it, and what people have to say and what the news reports have to say.'

'...And that's why God, I do understand and believe that this worlds destiny is not going to be determined by politicians and by news reporters, and those who stand in counsel with and take counsel from the wicked; this worlds destiny is not going to be determined by wicked people who takes counsel together against God and His Anointed, but the destiny

of this world is going to be determined by Your church God, by your people, by Your very own children who walk in understanding, they walk in the knowledge of who You really are and who they really are as Your children; they walk in the full knowledge of You, in the full knowledge of their God, and of themselves, and they will do exploits in that knowledge and in their God. The destiny of this world will be determined by them and by You and by nobody else Father God, I believe it, and I want to be, and I choose to be, and I will be a part of that God!'

*'Thank you Father that You are indeed at work within me **both to will <u>and to do</u>** Your good pleasure!'*

Listen don't let fear bind you up and dictate your actions, amen, rather let love rule you, and choose to yield and become part of what God wants to accomplish through you and through His true gospel in the earth today!

Can you now begin to see yourself, dare you see yourself, having great impact, because the truth of the gospel is rightly discerned in your heart, and you have come to a conclusion that the Word of God is true, that God is not a man that He should lie!

Listen God is not a man that He should tease and mock!

And why should He? God is light, and there is no darkness in Him whatsoever.

101

God is light! God is truth! God is love! There is no shadow of turning with Him.

That means He is trust-worthy. He can be fully trusted; He can be trusted to the uttermost!

We are dealing with God here after all, not Man, amen, not some figment of our imagination.

God is real, amen, and He is pure and Holy; He is love and He is God!

God is God, amen, and there is no other like Him!

Let me say again as I said in a previous chapter, the secret to the supernatural is: **Hearing with faith!**

In the light of that, let's just quickly turn also to Acts Chapter Fourteen then. Now this is Paul in action here.

Chapter 8

Hearing With Faith

Acts 14:1, *"Now at Iconium they entered together into the Jewish synagogue, **and so spoke** that a great many believed, both Jews and Greeks."*

Notice how Luke says that Paul, *"**spoke in such a way** that a great many believed; **he so spoke** that many believed"*

I believe what is written there in Romans 10:17 that, *"faith comes by hearing,"* but fear can also come by hearing, doubt can also come by hearing, unbelief can also come by hearing.

It is then obvious to me that if you want to produce faith in your hearers *then you need to speak in line with faith,* and not in a way that undermine the truth of the gospel found in the Scriptures. I mean, you need to boldly declare the faith of God revealed in the gospel, you need to **so speak *in such a way*** that faith is quickened; that faith is ignited!

How did you receive the Holy Spirit, how did you receive the evidence, or the working of power in your midst?

When you heard!

What did you hear?

How did you hear?

'Well, we heard conflicting rumors and hearsay, differing opinions you know; several different guys got up and spoke their minds about what THEY believed about the Holy Spirit.'

No! We heard from God. What God believe the Gospel is, and what God has to say about the Holy Spirit; what He believes and declares concerning the Holy Spirit and His ministry, and concerning receiving the Holy Spirit!

And so, what God believes I hear and I grasp, and that builds a faith in my spirit, and I receive by that faith built into my spirit.

*"Paul spoke **in such a way** that a great many believed."*

He *imparted* that same faith quickened within him to his hearers also.

Luke goes on to tell us there in that same scripture passage that while Paul was speaking there was a cripple man intently listening to what was being said; he hung on every word Paul was speaking.

Let's read it there. In Acts 14:7 it says that Paul and Barnabas *"were preaching the gospel."*

Verse 8, *"Now at Lystra there was a man sitting, who could not use his feet; and he was a cripple from birth, who had never walked."*

Verse 9, *"He listened to Paul speaking..."*

I want us to see where this man's miracle began to manifest.

Where did this man's miracle actually begin?

When Jesus Christ died in his place. When Jesus Christ took upon his own flesh our sickness, our disease, our infirmity; not just ours but this man's infirmary included, amen?! He took it upon Himself and He took it to the grave and left it there! And we were raised together with Him to newness of life, amen!

Now Paul came to this town, Lystra, and he preached **that** gospel. He preached **that** gospel **in such a way** that a cripple could sit there, who never even dreamt of walking, and as he listened, suddenly **that** gospel *brought faith into his heart.*

Verse 9 & 10, *"He listened to Paul speaking; and Paul, looking intently at him and seeing that he had faith to be made well, said to him in a loud voice, 'Stand upright on your feet.' And he sprang up and walked."*

Paul saw the moment for that miracle to manifest *when he saw the evidence of faith on that man's face.*

Paul could see something in this man's eyes and he knew that something supernatural, something beautiful to behold, was happening in this man's heart as he listened to the truth of the gospel and embraced it.

Paul was speaking about Jesus who *"went about doing good and healing the sick because God was with Him and He anointed Him"* (Acts 10:38).

This man's response wasn't just neutral. And he obviously wasn't just sitting there all religious like some dead beat dog, or like a bump on a log either, thinking to himself, *'I wonder when this service is going to be over so I can get out of here.'* I mean he was not sitting there, bored out of his mind! He wasn't just sitting there with his spirit in neutral mode!

No man, he was fully engaged in what was said; *"He **listened** to Paul speaking..."*

And let me tell you, he was obviously not sitting there all cynical either, judging and criticizing everything Paul was saying. No, he wasn't doing that, but instead this man knew that there was an opportunity in this gospel for him. He knew that this gospel uniquely presented him with an opportunity to experience the supernatural.

And he sat there, and intently *"He **listened** to Paul speaking,"* and he wanted it. He wanted what Paul was talking about, *and in what was said he saw that he could have it*
106

*"He **listened** to Paul speaking; and Paul, looking intently at him and seeing that he had faith to be made well, said to him in a loud voice, 'Stand upright on your feet.'*

He was obviously not sitting there all arrogant and thinking, *'Hmm, you know, this man doesn't know what he is talking about. He just doesn't know how long I've been crippled.'*

No, it says, *"And he sprang up and walked."*

And I want to encourage you who are reading this book right now, **don't just sit there and be neutral!** You will never receive from God with that attitude! Don't think about what others are saying. Their opinions don't matter! Don't worry about what others will think about you and say about you. **Your miracle is important to God if it's important to you!**

Remember blind Bartimaeus (Mark10:46-52)? He only heard the reports of Jesus, and he never even saw Him because he was blind, but the reports were enough. He heard those reports, *and faith comes by hearing.* **There was enough in what he heard to awaken and quicken faith within him.** He embraced it as the truth, *and faith began to break through in his spirit,* and suddenly he had a new ambition in his life. He knew in his spirit that it was going to be possible for me, through this man Jesus Christ, to see again, for I have come to believe that He is indeed the son of David, the Messiah sent from Heaven; the Son of God! And an opportunity presented itself and Bartimaeus had to not take that opportunity for granted, but he had to take it boldly! People even tried to quiet him down because he was making a noise, *but a determination born of faith possessed his heart.* **He knew that this faith is a persuasion from God.** It is not just a nice idea, not just a nice positive thought, *it's a persuasion that arrests and grips the spirit, and you know that you know that you know that there is healing for me; the supernatural is available for me.* And Bartimaeus cried out all the more and would not be denied. He cried out to Jesus, *'Son of David, have mercy on me!'* And Jesus pinpointing his faith said, *'What exactly do you want from Me?'* And he said, *'Jesus, that I might see.'* **Upon hearing this, Jesus released his healing.** He said to him, *'Go, your faith has made you well.'*

Listen to me, I don't care if you get offended at me right now, and I don't care what anyone has tried to tell you, *I care enough about you to tell you the truth:* **Your faith has something to do with the supernatural!**

You see if it was all just up to God, and the supernatural was just God's business, in God's domain only, then we would see the supernatural happen automatically; we would see it happening around us all the time! But the truth is, your faith has something to do with you experiencing the supernatural.

Don't get me wrong, I am not saying that God cannot do it that way, that God cannot arbitrarily intervene supernaturally by His grace, He can and He does, amen, it's not His usual modes operandi; He doesn't usually operate that way.

I say again: **Your faith comes into play when it comes to you experiencing the supernatural.**

Your faith response to what you have heard in the truth of the gospel can activate the grace of God!

We read again and again in the Scriptures that Jesus commended *their* faith; He commended people's faith.

What did those people's faith reveal to Jesus?

It revealed their appreciation, their praise of His integrity.

To exhibit faith is to praise and highly esteem the integrity of God!

My faith is the evidence of my heart saying to God, *'You are not a failure God! You are the Great and Mighty God who is love personified; the Almighty One, and I praise and exalt You as my DADDY and as my GOD because I believe the gospel! You can do anything God; You can do it!'*

And you know what, God is pleased by that faith (Hebrews 11:6).

You see if I can have the favor of God, then I know that I am going to have Him on my side. Then I know that if God fights for me, who can be against me. Who can fight God, if God is for me?!

Listen I have news for you: In Christ Jesus God Himself has revealed to us that we have Him and that we have His favor, amen!

Faith knows that God is for me.

Let me say that again: Faith knows and is persuaded that God is for me.

There might be financial situations against me, there might be sickness against me, there might be all kinds of things in the natural against me, BUT GOD IS FOR ME!

GOD IS FOR YOU TOO!

GOD IS FOR YOU!

Say it with me: GOD IS FOR ME!

Now say it like you believe it: GOD IS FOR ME!

Listen; HE TRULY IS! Hallelujah!

GOD IS FOR YOU!

Father I praise You and I thank you that You are for us!

You are not the one who is against us; You are not the thief that comes to steal, kill, and destroy, but You are for us; You have come to give us life, and that more abundantly in Jesus!

Father, thank you that You came to give us life more abundantly!

Thank you Jesus!

You have conquered!

Father I praise You, You are on my side!

You have conquered in Jesus and You are on my side!

You are the God of the impossible!

Nothing is too difficult for You!

Hallelujah!

Nothing is too difficult for Him!

So, Paul saw that this man had faith to be healed through what he heard in the gospel and Paul responded, and so with a loud faith filled voice, his own faith being quickened and activated also, from that faith alive in him also Paul commanded the man to stand up straight on his feet, and faith connected with faith, and the power of God was released, and received, and the man sprang up and he walked.

Would you agree that that is the evidence of the supernatural?! It cannot be explained any other way. It's not merely a placebo effect as some idiots want to claim these days, its supernatural, amen?!

That's the only accurate explanation of what took place here! And I too have many faith stories in my own life also as evidence to back this up, but again, I don't have time to share them with you right now, because it is not about you thinking, *'Wow, this brother Rudi is really something, isn't he?!'* No I am not! And what I need you to grasp and understand is that the same gospel that works for me will work for you **if you would receive it as the truth and finally take your eyes off of people and fix it on the God who has revealed Himself, and His love for you, so clearly in the gospel.**

The supernatural is real and available in Jesus Name, not just to some of us, but to all those who believe!

Jesus himself said as much in Mark Chapter 16:17-18, *"And these signs shall accompany the believers: In My name they will cast out devils; they will speak in other tongues; they will pick up serpents (by accident) and if they drink any deadly thing (accidentally or being forced to by others), it shall not hurt them; they*

112

will lay their hands on the sick, and they will recover."

Now, I also want you to notice that Paul didn't say, *'Well, you know, if you go and confess all your sins, and for the next 3 months come to my office and I'll counsel you, and I'll do some inner healing things on you and help you get rid of all the disappointments of your past, then maybe you'll qualify, maybe, we don't know, but maybe, you know we never know, because God's ways are mysterious ways, you know, His thoughts are above our thoughts, so we don't know what's going to happen, but we'll give you a chance, you know, if you come to our office like I said and we counsel you, and try and help you get rid of all your problems, you know, all those things you have inherited, because you know, your parents sinned, and your great grandparents, you know, they sinned, so you have inherited a lot of nonsense, and we have to first help you get rid of all of that before we can maybe help you...'*

No man, Paul didn't say any of that, because you see **Paul believed in our original design and in our true identity re-revealed in Jesus Christ; He knew the New Creation created in Christ Jesus settled everything; *it settled it all!*** In the mind of God the New Creation created there in Christ Jesus and His work of redemption *settled it all,* because as far as He is concerned it has already been settled there from the very beginning, *and nothing that happened to us in time could unsettle that.*

The Fall itself was not enough to unsettle the mind of God made up concerning who we really are!

Paul fully understood that God's ministry towards us is not based upon the performance or the failure of our great granddad. It is solely based upon God's own performance in the Son; in Christ Jesus.

And therefore according to Paul in 2 Corinthians 5:17, *"If any man is in Christ,"* and we all were and are, amen, **we were placed in Christ by God's own doing.**

Jesus represented the whole human race, and what He did, *He did for all.* If He did not include the whole human race *then who did He die for?* **If He did not die for all, then He did not die for any!**

He died for us all amen!

And so Paul says, *"And **THEREFORE** if any man is in Christ, he is a New Creation; the old things have passed away, **behold now the new has come; the entire cosmos has been renewed**"*

He goes on to say in verse 18, *"**All this is from God, <u>who through Christ reconciled us all to Himself</u>,** and He has given this to us* (who know and understand and believe these things) *He has given it to us, as a ministry to others; the ministry of reconciliation..."*

You see; that whole record of human history, that false evidence, that whole lie we have believed about ourselves, and also then lived as a result, from generation to generation, all because of Adam and Eve's deception, their embrace of the lie – all that **passed away** through the death of Jesus. His blood, **which cries better things concerning us** than that of Abel, *deals once and for all with your past and cancels it for good!*

Praise God!

Listen I say again: If we want to operate in the supernatural, we need to get rid of our funny doctrines; our weird and strange religious beliefs we have held on to since the Fall, and in light of the Fall. They make no real sense when they are challenged in the light of God's revelation of Himself, and of us, in Christ Jesus!

If we want to begin entering the supernatural we have to begin first with rightly handling the Word of Truth; the gospel of our salvation which already took place - It already happened, amen, in Jesus Christ.

Many ministers and ministries of today have adopted all kinds of Psychological ideas like inner-healing and all the different counseling patterns for it, to take people into their past and getting them into some kind of emotional deliverance. But you see; Man is spirit, soul, and body, and as long as ministry is engaged in the soul realm, it is ineffective, and it will remain ineffective!

Listen Jesus was the first born from the dead, and on that basis, on that merit, we have a sure word to deliver to this world; we have a gospel of truth, absolute truth, which persuades people. And we are not merely talking intellect and mind over matter now, and willpower, no, we are talking **spirit reality.**

When we are dealing with the gospel we are dealing with Spirit dimension and Spirit power; we are engaging the very power of God as we present to people the true gospel of God and the truth contained in that gospel. And Jesus said, *"You will know that truth and that truth will set you free!"* Why is that? Because we are dealing with God now, **with the very power of God unto salvation,** and not merely with insignificant little man-made theories and teachings and doctrine and psychobabble!

You see Jesus' resurrection meant our resurrection, we were raised with Him to newness of life, and on the basis of His resurrection, on the basis of that life released there in the resurrection **unto all of us** we have a sure word to this world; a gospel that **supernaturally goes right into the heart** of even the hardest sinner, and suddenly in his spirit he realizes, *'There is hope for me after all! There is salvation for me, and there is healing for me! I too can be made whole in my embrace of the gospel!"*

I can even be cripple from my mother's womb, it makes no difference, just like that young man in Paul's audience in Acts 14, and we can all imagine just how often he resented the day that he was born, and the ridicule he must have suffered as a child, and we can imagine how many religious questions might have haunted and plagued his mind, *'Why am I like this?! Why am I in this condition? Was it my mother who sinned, or did my father do the sinning,'* **but the gospel cleared all that up for him when it was so accurately presented by Paul,** *and faith came into his heart,* a faith that says to him and lets him know in his own heart that, *'God is not to blame for my condition. All the questions and lies I have believed and embraced, which has plagued me for so long,* **they are all undone in the light of His love,** <u>**in the light of the truth of the gospel**</u>, *and therefore I too can be made whole, because I too was raised to newness of life in Jesus!'*

You see Paul came not to try and explain psychologically why this man had that condition, why that kind of suffering was placed upon him as a burden to bear, no, Paul came with the truth of the gospel to undo every lie, every demonic religious deception; he came to manifest the glory of God and to undo the work of evil, and he was bold about it, because he knew that that crippled state this man was in was not just natural and had to be accepted as natural, but Paul knew that it was an evil, it was evil at work; the product of demon activity –

adversarial forces at work in this man's life. Paul knew and understood that it was the work of the thief which comes to steal, kill, and destroy, but that Jesus had come to give even this man, life more abundantly, because Jesus was sent to heal all who are oppressed of the devil; of their adversary. Paul knew that as he came with the open statement of the truth, with the bold deceleration of the gospel, he would be able to undo all the works of evil and that he would be able to heal all who are oppressed by an entity of evil, because God is with him, just as He was with Jesus (Acts 10:38).

Paul didn't come to just write a nice intellectual little essay on Divine healing and in there try to explain why some are healed, and why some aren't healed. Why sometimes it works and other times it doesn't turn out so well and it doesn't work. He didn't try and explain the supernatural and butch it up, undermining faith, and effectively blocking the supernatural and shutting down its manifestation. No, for him this whole thing went beyond intellectual arguments. He didn't try and discuss the supernatural and explain it in human terms, explaining it away, because a greater conviction ruled in his heart and he was convinced, he was persuaded inside his inner-man, inside his spirit that Jesus fulfilled the just requirements, **He restored it all,** everything Man lost in the Fall. When He became a curse both the Law and the Fall was fulfilled, **it came to a final conclusion and end; it's time was**

up! And so the Scriptures boldly declare that, *"By His stripes we are healed!"*

Jesus took our sickness and disease upon Him, *every effect of the Fall,* **and He effectively canceled it in His death, and He buried it and left it in the grave,** *and then He raised us up to newness of life with Him!*

Listen you don't need to be too clever to discern the difference between a curse and a blessing, and Paul knew that sickness was a curse; it was not a blessing.

Religious people have tried to turn sickness and disease into a blessing, you know, *'Well, it's a blessing in one way, you see, because through this blessing I am getting closer to God.'* But that's a lie!

Listen; God doesn't bless in disguise! **When He blesses** *He blesses through the knowledge of the truth of His Word.*

There is so much blessing in this Word of the gospel, no sickness could ever add to its joy, oh, it could try and diminish its joy and take away from its joy, but it cannot add anything to you!

Stop worrying and agonizing over YOUR faith, trying to figure out if it is big enough or strong enough or mature enough, or whether you even have enough faith and all such silly notions people talk about. Get your eyes off of yourself! Stop all your questioning and self-examination and begin to look away unto Jesus, the Author and Finisher of faith.

I am so glad that the gospel doesn't demand faith; **it supplies it!**

It matters not what we believe, it matters only what God believes, *and God believes fully in that which was accomplished in Jesus.* **God believes in His Son's successful achievement on our behalf. God believes in that work of redemption.**

That faith of God **defines reality!**

God's belief **defines faith** for us!

I am so glad we don't have to try and define it on our own.

And I'm so glad we don't have to try and believe on our own and come up with faith; a faith of our own making!

God is the source of faith; Faith is sourced in God, amen, He supplies it. Faith comes from Him, not us!

All we need is the faith of God; not our faith!

That faith comes by hearing the gospel.

As I said before: I am so glad the gospel doesn't demand faith; **it supplies it!**

The faith of God is imparted through the gospel and becomes your faith.

When you hear with faith the truth of the gospel, the blessing of God will begin to manifest in your life; you'll begin to be a blessed one. You'll begin to know the blessing of God's favor in your life. You'll begin to know what it means to walk free from religion, no longer under God's supposed frown; His suspicion and wrath and judgment, but you'll be walking under the smile of Abba Father; under the shadow of the Almighty, under that shadow of the Holy Spirit, knowing your Daddy's smile and His favor.

So, *"Paul preached **in such a way**."* And if we want to discover how Paul preached then we have to go and discover what the content was of Paul's ministry. If you go and read the letters that Paul wrote to the Church, you'll discover something about his preaching. There was something mighty, something powerful and glorious that was stirring in the heart of Paul, there was a burning passion in his heart; he wasn't just doing little religious talks here and there to impress the religious, to try and impress the multitudes and to try and get the nations to embrace an interesting new little philosophy of Man, *but he came filled with passion to fully preach and make known the gospel of God, the truth of that gospel, the love of God so clearly revealed there.* He came in the demonstration of power and of Spirit, *for the Holy Spirit was within him.*

Paul writes later on in 1 Corinthians 9:24 and he says, *"Don't run aimlessly, but **so** run (run in such a way) that you may obtain success."*

There is a lot of running going on, there is a lot of religious zeal and performance going on; *'We're doing our little religious things as well'* So, here we go and we have our little church service, but is there any merit, any evidence of the supernatural, any real value, any real gain for God in that service?

But, *"...**so** run,"* says Paul, and I believe that *"...**so** run"* begins with, *"...**so** believe"* and *"...**so** preach"*

*"We believe and **so** we speak!"* - 2 Corinthians 4:13

If you want to hear my conversation, the only thing I will let you know and come in agreement with is the testimony of Jesus Christ. I will not emphasize my experience in the flesh over what took place in Him on my behalf and was revealed in Him concerning me! See, my conversation will be a faith conversation, not a flesh conversation. I prefer a faith conversation over a flesh conversation any day. So, if you want to engage me in conversation to locate me; to see where I am at spiritually, I am not going to go into great detail in my conversation and tell you how sick I feel, and the record and the history of this particular sickness, and the history of that particular situation, and what the medical profession and science has to say about this and what they have to say about that!

Now don't get me wrong, I am not against the medical profession, there are some great doctors and nurses out there trying their best to help people, and many of them are among my friends even, and if I need to I will go see a doctor, and have a procedure done, if it is absolutely necessary, *but I will maintain my faith focus and conversation;* **I will keep my eyes on Jesus,** *the Author and Finisher of faith. In Him as my healer and the sustainer of my life, I put my trust and rest secure!*

Listen; I will not exalt my experience and place it above the Word of God. I will glorify God, rather than glorify my situation and see it as greater than God. God is greater than anything that might try and come against me! His love for me is greater! His power is greater! I believe and **so** I speak!

Romans 8:31-39

*"What then shall we **say** in all of this?"*

"Since God is for us, who can be against us! He who did not spare His own life even, but gave it up for us all in Jesus the Son, will He then not also give us all other things, just as He gave Himself as a gift in the Son! God has identified us as His own, who shall bring any charge against us so as to try and disqualify us!? No one can even point a finger to try and shame us; He has justified us! Who is there

123

left to condemn us? It certainly is not Christ who condemns us, He as our intercessor died and was raised from the dead, and even represents us right now, seated in the bosom of the Father, and therefore also in a place of authority at the right hand of God! What and who can possibly separate us from the love of God for us demonstrated in Christ Jesus!? Can tribulation, or distress, or persecution, or famine, or nakedness, or peril, or any other kind of weapon accomplish such a feet!? By no means! In spite of these things, yes, even while going through these things, we remain secure, more than conquerors; unable to be defeated by these things, all through Him who loves us! For I am convinced, by the demonstration of His love for me in Jesus Christ, that neither death, nor life, nor angelic beings, demon powers or political principalities, nor things present, (nothing known to us at this time), nor things to come, (even in the unknown near or distant future), nor any other kind of powers, (no dimension of any calculation in time or space), nor any device yet to be invented, has what it takes to separate us from the love of God! What was revealed by God in Jesus Christ concerning us, and concerning His love for us, is and remains our ultimate authority, no matter what we find ourselves facing!"

*"We believe and **so** we speak!"* - 2 Corinthians 4:13

This reminds me of one more miraculous testimony I suddenly feel compelled to share with you: One of the young men associated with our ministry, called me last night. He is still working to earn a living for himself and his young family while their ministry is growing, but on his time off away from work he and his wife are starting little home groups in the neighborhoods all over the town where they live. And so, last night on the phone he shared with me that they were ministering the night before in one of these little home groups to a baby who was coughing constantly, and he and his wife took authority over that cough and the condition causing it, even though they didn't even know what it was exactly that caused the cough, but in Jesus Name they commanded it to stop, and it did.

'But this is the strange thing that happened,' he said, *'In just a few minutes the baby began to cough again, and the cough was so bad this time that it became quite a distraction to people's focus and interrupted the spiritual environment and all the things, good things that was happening supernaturally in the spirit realm in people's hearts, because of that Spirit-environment.'*

'Now we had just prayed a few minutes ago, and the thing stopped,' he said to me, *'But now it was back again, so I thought to myself: Wow what do we do now? And then I realized, and this must have been supernaturally by a gift of the Holy Spirit imparted to me at that moment,*

I realized,' he said, *'that something must have happened in that mother's heart in those few minutes since we last prayed and the cough stopped, so I immediately spoke to the mother and said to her, 'Maria, I want you to **confirm, verbally,** not the fears of your heart, **but the faith of your heart,** right now.'* He said, *'I said to her, 'Say with me: I believe that my baby is healed right now!'.* He told me how Maria looked up at him as if she was arrested in her spirit right then and there by the Holy Spirit and interrupted in her negative spiral of thoughts.

'And she locked eyes with me,' he said, *'and got up from where she was sitting and stood upright on her feet, and said, 'I fully believe and declare right now that my baby is healed!'*

'And guess what,' he said, *'It was simply astonishing to watch what happened next. That baby stopped coughing right there and then, and never coughed again!'*

He told me how they even took that mother and child home later on in the evening to another neighborhood clear across town to the next town over where she was from, and that child never coughed again, not even once!

*"We believe and **so** we speak!"* - 2 Corinthians 4:13

See I believe that there is something powerful attached to the confession of your mouth.

126

What the heart is full of, the mouth will run over with! So, don't let Satan hijack your mouth because you allow fear to fester in your heart, because whether it is faith or fear you confess, it will control and affect your life!

Being filled with fear is just having faith in the wrong thing. Giving voice to your fears is putting that negative faith into action, so it is better to shut your mouth until you can get your eyes back on Jesus where they belong and your heart in a place of faith, but make no mistake, you cannot just guard your words, you have to guard your heart with all diligence, because with the heart one believes and *therefore* with the mouth confession is made unto either salvation or destruction!

Quite often you will find that without a firm verbal confession of faith inspired by a true conviction of heart in the truth as it is revealed in the gospel *no breakthrough will be had in an adverse situation.*

That's why we are encouraged in the book of Hebrews to *"hold fast to the confession of your faith without wavering!"* - Hebrews 10:23

Romans 10:8 states, *"The Word is near you, on your lips **and in your heart!**"*

That's why it says in verse 10,

*"For with the heart one believes **and (therefore)** with the mouth confession is made unto salvation!"*

*"We believe and **so** we speak!"* - 2 Corinthians 4:13

I really do believe that there is something powerful attached to the confession of your mouth.

And no, I don't mean for you to now go overboard, thinking that every little thing you or others say will affect your life or theirs, and so you go around correcting every little word coming out of someone's mouth. That is just stupid.

Although, it is true that your mouth does reveal where you are at in your heart, and therefore, listening every now and then to your own words coming out of your mouth, could help you get your eyes off of your circumstance and put it back on Jesus where it belongs.

And yes, you do have to watch your mouth when it comes to other people as well. Sometimes we do say the darndest things that end up negatively impacting or severely hurting other people. So, we do have to be careful with our words and guard what we think and say, **but there is a big difference** *between innocent casual conversation and something that is said deliberately, in a flippant manner, or spoken with conviction from the heart.*

Listen; when it comes to the powerful spiritual forces that affect our lives, **only what you say from the heart,** *only what you really believe with your heart and then as if in automatic*

128

mode declare over yourself and others with your mouth has a real and powerful impact in the spirit realm and in life.

Don't let it be negative destructive forces you put into motion in your life and others, rather put your eyes on Jesus, focus your faith in the truth of the gospel, and as the gospel impacts your heart and impart the faith of God there, let it come out of your mouth with conviction. Let the faith of God find voice in you!

The very creative power of God is invested **in His Word; *in the truth of the gospel.***

*"**The Word** is near you, **in your heart, and in your mouth!**" - Romans 10:8*

*"**That Word - The gospel** is the power of God unto salvation!" - Romans 1:16*

You see; if it was all just God's responsibility and we had no part in it, then we can all just go around with our hands in our pockets and say, *'Well, God, bless me. It's all up to Him, you know, He is doing it all, it's all His part, I have no part to play in it, He's doing it.'* And then when we see nothing happening we angrily say, *'God, why aren't you doing it for me today? I asked You to do it and You're not doing anything!'* As if God is our servant now, or our pet monkey, or something like that, and we just call on Him and He's going to take action and come and do it.

No listen; **My faith and your faith has something to do with the manifestation of God's power in our lives!**

And that faith is not just a silent thing!

When Paul writes to the churches in Colossians and in Ephesians he says, *"I thank God that I've heard of your faith."*

You see their faith was loud, and the reports about it traveled a long way; their faith traveled many miles, and it came to the ears of Paul.

Hey, people need to hear about your faith! When you visit people don't talk about your problems, talk about your faith. They really aren't all that interested in your problems anyway, and even if they are, they can only give you sympathy, that's all, and that empathy and sympathy can't really help you, *but it may even take you to your grave sooner.*

Sympathy doesn't really strengthen you; *only faith can strengthen you!*

Paul said to the Ephesian believers in Ephesians 3:14-16, *"I desire that **Christ may dwell (abide) in your hearts** through faith."* He says *"I desire that according to the gospel, or through the gospel, through the riches of His glory revealed there, **that you may be strengthened with might By His Spirit in your inner-being**."*

Hallelujah!

130

People want to hear about your faith; they need to hear about your faith. And you know what your faith is? It's a boasting. And so I begin to boast about Jesus. You see because *"if my righteousness is a product of my keeping the Law, then I would have reason to boast in myself,"* says Paul, but now because my righteousness is a product of Jesus, therefore I boast in Him; I would much rather boast in **HIM! I glorify Him, I lift Him up, I exalt His name in front of the whole world and I want to tell the world of this great salvation, of this great miracle power that is still evident today!**

Let's go to Acts 10 quickly. This is what I want you to see: *I want you to see that the Holy Spirit is always ready to respond. The grace of God is always ready to respond! God is not reluctant;* ***He in His grace stands ready to respond to the Word!***

*"**I am watching over My Word to perform it.**"*
- Jeremiah 1:12

Chapter 9

"I Will Manifest Myself To You!"

Here in Acts 10 Peter visits the household of Cornelius.

Verse 34,

"And Peter opened his mouth and said..."

I am so glad that Peter didn't sit around and talk about the weather. And he didn't start in on His own opinions about this situation he found himself in either; he didn't begin speaking from his own religious beliefs and voice his own prejudice against gentiles, but instead he got on with it; he got on with the job and got straight to the point.

*"He opened his mouth **and said...**"*

Listen; We need to begin to be so saturated with the Word of God; with the content and clarity of the gospel, that when we open our mouths to speak, people begin to take out their pens to write down what is being said, because it is so simple and to the point and yet so profound and impacting that they cannot help but take notes. As for instance in this Scripture, because obviously someone was listening to Peter speak and got what he had to say, and the whole experience was so powerful that they wrote it down for us, so that we may also read and grasp and experience the same things.

"And Peter opened his mouth and said: Truly I perceive that God shows no partiality, but in every nation, anyone who respects and appreciates Him and therefore responds to Him accordingly, is acceptable to Him."

He says in verse 36,

"You know the Word which He sent to Israel, preaching the good news of peace by Jesus Christ."

He goes on to say in verse 37,

*"(For in case you haven't heard it,) this then is the word which was proclaimed throughout all Judea, beginning from Galilee after the baptism which John preached: (This is the content of their gospel) It is all about **how God anointed Jesus of Nazareth with the Holy Spirit and with power; how he went about doing good and healing all who were oppressed by the devil, for God was with him.**"*

You know, the Holy Spirit made Jesus' ministry public. Without the Holy Spirit there is no public ministry. Without the Holy Spirit there is no real ministry at all.

You see Jesus was just a carpenter. Oh, don't get me wrong, He was the Son of God; God in the flesh, Emanuel – God with us. But in His daily routine, as a Man, as a human being like the rest of us, He was just involved in carpentry and meditating on the Scriptures, but there came a day when the Holy Spirit came upon Him with power, and that day made a distinct difference in His life; it thrust Him forth into ministry. And Jesus began to work together and flow with the Holy Spirit, and the Holy Spirit brought His ministry to others into a new dimension.

Have you noticed how the whole Trinity was involved here: *"How God the Father anointed Jesus, the Son, with the Holy Spirit and with power?"*

In John's account of this event in Jesus' life John wrote how the Father anointed His Son. He spoke out of heaven and He says: *"This is My beloved Son in whom I am well pleased,"* and the Holy Spirit fell upon (or ignited) Him (from within). And so as a result of this Jesus could no longer sit still in his earthly father's little factory, or His heavenly Father's factory for that matter. We read how He went around preaching the good news message that the kingdom of God is at hand, in fact He said that it is within us, and then we also read how He not only preached these things but demonstrated it. His message stirred faith in the hearts of the people and so He went about not only preaching but healing the sick and casting out devils. The Holy Spirit all the while working with Him from within Him by confirming the word which He preached with signs and wonders following the word which He preached. The Scriptures says, *"He went around doing good, healing all who were oppressed of the devil, for God was with Him."*

You see the Holy Spirit has wings, and He will begin to move you; He will begin to stir and get that word which is deposited and lodged within your spirit to become mobile.

"He went about doing good!"

It does not say: *"He went about doing good, breaking people's arms and what not, saying: 'God's going to teach you something through this!' And putting cancer on people, saying: 'Just hang in there, God wants to teach you.'* No! It doesn't say that! It says, *"He went about doing good, **healing <u>all</u> who were oppressed by the devil**"*

This scripture clearly suggests that all sickness is the fruit of some kind of oppression going on; some kind of spiritual and mental oppression. John said as much in John 10:10, he says it is the work of a thief. He said, *"The thief comes to steal, destroy and kill, but not Jesus. Jesus comes to give us life and that more abundantly!"*

Listen: **God is not the thief! God doesn't come to steal, destroy or kill! God doesn't**

come to put sickness on anyone, because God wants you well!

God says, ***'The thief came to steal, but I came to give you life and that more abundantly!'***

I really do believe that health is part of that abundant life which God desires for you and for me and for everyone!

I am aware of the fact that many other people might believe differently and preach differently, but as for me, I am going to **so** believe and **so** preach.

Every now and then I hear from somebody that wants to tell me, *'Well, WE never see the supernatural manifest in our midst.'* You know why that is: It's because they never preach it, because they don't believe it!

Listen; It will be unto you, according to your faith.

So if you want to believe in sickness and go ahead and get sick and stay sick, you just go right ahead, but as for me, I am going to believe the fact that God does want me well; God does want me healthy. I am going to believe God's Word, I'm going to believe the gospel, I'm going to believe in health and trust God for it!

But let's get back to our scripture passage.

Acts 10:38, "**God anointed Jesus of Nazareth with the Holy Spirit and with power; and he went about doing good and healing all who were oppressed by the devil, for God was with him.**"

Verse 39,

"And we are witnesses to all that He did both in the country of the Jews and in Jerusalem. And there they put Him to death by hanging Him on a tree, **but God raised Him from the dead on the third day and revealed Him to be the Preeminent One, sent and meant to lead us all.**"

In verse 41 Peter goes on to say,

"God made Him manifest, not to all the people, but to us who believe in Him. We were chosen by God as witnesses of these things. We ate and drank with him after he rose from the dead. He himself commanded us to preach to the people, and to testify that He is the One ordained by God to be the judge of the living and the dead (and thus to declare them all forgiven and innocent and set them all free)."

Verse 43,

"To Him all the prophets bear witness that everyone who believes in Him experiences not only forgiveness of sins, but a release from it, through His name."

It is interesting to note in verse 41 that *"God made Him manifest, not to all the people, but to us who believe in Him..."*

So why did Jesus not make Himself manifest to all the people? Because in John 14 He said: *"The world will no longer see Me, but you will see Me"*

So what is so special about them? The answer is in John 14:23, He says, *"If any person loves Me they will treasure My word, and My Father will love them, and We will come to them and make Our home with them."*

So, if you want to have Jesus manifest His resurrection to you, love His word, treasure His word, amen?!

Another translation of Acts 10:43 read:

"To Him all the prophets bear witness that everyone who believes in Him **receives** *forgiveness of sins through His name."*

Everyone who believes in Him **receives.**

"How did you receive?" - Galatians 3:5

"By hearing <u>with faith</u>."

Hebrews 4:2, says about the people in Moses' day: *"The good news they heard did not benefit them;* **not being met with faith** *in those who heard it."*

So there in Acts 10, how are these people going to receive the forgiveness of their sins?

By hearing with faith.

You see the Word, the gospel has to be met with faith. And faith comes when the gospel comes. It literally gets imparted by the Word and by the Holy Spirit who watches over that Word to make it come alive in us! So you literally have to reject the faith that comes to you when the gospel comes to you, in order to not get influenced by it.

Now verse 44 says, *"While Peter was still saying this, the Holy Spirit fell on all who heard the word."*

Obviously that only happened because they embraced the Word, instead of arguing with it and rejecting it.

I cannot over emphasize this fact: *If you want to begin to encounter and experience the supernatural in your life,* **begin to really hear the Word! Begin to make the Word of God a priority in your life,** and not your favorite TV program, and that nice magazine, or blog or Social Media outlet, not even that political discussion and point of view you have become so enamored by and caught up in, *but rather, open your ears and your heart and your mind to God and say in your heart to God:* **'God, I'm listening for Your voice; I'm tuning my spirit to hear the Rhema of God in the Logos.'**

140

And so then as that word begins to live in my inner-man the Holy Spirit comes with the supernatural and He makes it a reality to me; He brings it into reality, amen!

The Greek word 'Logos' represents the eternal Word of God, and the 'Rhema' speaks of revelation into the Logos. It means that the 'Logos' now comes alive to me through revelation, through insight and revelation into it by the intimate voice of God; fresh communication within my spirit coming to me in the here and now from the indwelling Holy Spirit.

Listen; **Make room for the Holy Spirit in your life! Create an abiding place for Him in your heart! Begin to give the truth of the gospel a place of absolute priority and authority in your life.**

Okay, you can go read the rest of that passage in Acts 10 for yourself if you want to, but let me just take you briefly to Hebrews 2:1-4 in closing.

Chapter 10

Pay Closer Attention

Hebrews 2:1-4,

"Therefore we must pay the more earnest heed to what we've heard..."

Another translation says,

"We must pay closer attention to what we have heard..."

What you hear precedes the supernatural in your life, but your lack of attention - your lack of commitment to what you hear - will rob you of the supernatural!

This word, *"attention"* literally means: **To become addicted to.**

The writer of Hebrews says, "*We must pay the more earnest heed to what we've heard* (we must become addicted to it) *lest we drift away from it."*

Verse 2,

"For if the message declared by angels was valid, and every transgression or violation of it, every disobedience to it received its own just

retribution, how shall we escape (sin or sickness or whatever other onslaught that comes against us) *...how shall we escape* (these things) *...how shall we escape* (the effects or the consequences of it) *...how shall we escape **if we neglect such a great salvation?!**"*

You see; the faith that comes to us and gets imparted through the gospel of our salvation **celebrates a dimension of life given to humanity that exceeds every bonsai boundary and restriction that we've imagined, inherited or created!**

"I have come that you might have life and have it more abundantly!" - Jesus (John 10:10)

That is why the writer of Hebrews continues by saying:

"This great salvation was declared at first by the Lord, and it was attested to us by those who heard Him, while God himself also bore witness, by signs and wonders and various miracles, and by gifts from the Holy Spirit, distributed according to His own will."

If it was the will and desire of the Holy Spirit to distribute those gifts then, and it surely was, then it is still His will and desire to distribute the same gifts today still, and whatever gifts might be needed now.

He hasn't changed, amen!

God hasn't changed, amen!

Jesus Christ, the same, yesterday, today, tomorrow, and forever, amen!

How did God respond?

He responded with the supernatural.

Why did God respond with the supernatural?

To bear witness to the integrity and greatness of our salvation!

God responded with the supernatural to bear witness to the integrity of the Word that we've heard!

Listen; God wants to confirm His Word with signs and wonders.

You see God wants me and you to take a hold of an understanding that will introduce us to life more abundantly and to the supernatural.

Why? Because the understanding of the natural man *is limited and flawed.* Listen carefully to what I am saying now, because there are two kinds of understanding. The understanding of the natural man is called: Reason. And reason is the child of your senses. Reason is the product of your education through your senses, through what you experience in life, good or bad, *and it is deeply flawed.*

But God wants to bring all of us to a new kind of understanding.

He says in verse 1 of Hebrews 11, *"And now faith is the substance of things hoped for, the very evidence of unseen realities; the surety of things not seen yet."*

Verse 3,

"By faith we understand that the world was created by the very Word of God, so that what is seen was made out of things which do not appear, but are real none the less."

Faith takes you and links you to the invisible reality of God's Word, and the reality of God Himself.

God is eager to call those things that are not as though they are, as though they were already, because as far as He is concerned, they exist already!

As far as He is concerned it is a settled matter; a done deal!

He wants us to come into agreement with Him as well and consider it as good as done!

So, God wants to call those things that be not as though they were, in your life.

There are certain areas in your life that you have submitted to, strongholds if you will, areas of bondage, certain habits, like smoking.

You do understand don't you, that smoking is this little habit that you begin to yield to and eventually completely submit to, and it becomes very convenient to you. You see you begin to accommodate a thief in your life. Oh sure, you know that this thing destroys your health and you are going to die many years younger than you need to. Oh you know already and are well aware of the fact that many die of lung cancer because of smoking, but somehow you have come to the conclusion to ignore all those statistics and hold on to this little habit that has now become a big one. I mean somehow it has become so nice to hold on to this little habit that you totally ignore its claim upon your life. Like a little parasite it is slowly but surely draining your physical life-source.

Some enjoy their little magazines and their little dirty books, and their little naughty television programs, and their little Internet pornography behind closed doors, and their other little things that, you know, rob them somehow in some seemingly small insignificant little way. It really is amazing how the enemy of your soul can introduce a little thief and make it look like a friend, and so, we have kind of welcomed it, and we somewhat enjoy its presence in our lives, but through the gospel of truth, the gospel of my salvation in Christ Jesus, I've realized that it's an enemy in my life, it's a foe, and I desire to be set free from it, to shake of its shackles and chains from my life, I desire to walk in this new realm of life available to me in

Jesus Christ, and I desire to walk in that anointing that breaks the yoke, so I can be free indeed, so I can be a child of the Most High God, not just in name only, but for real!

Now this gospel that came to you in this book, and which you can find in my other books already mentioned earlier on, is God's guarantee to you that if you have an ear to hear and a heart to believe, God himself is ready to confirm His Word to you.

Whatever ties you up in bondage today, whether it is sickness, or disease, infirmary, a habit of some kind, financial problems, sin of any kind, whatever it may be ...and maybe you have gone to church many times, or all your life for that matter, and you have done some religious things, but you have never experienced the "New Birth," or whatever you want to call that transformation experience and encounter of the real and living God, listen, you, yes you can experience that, you can experience Him today and be free, right now, right there where you are sitting and reading this book!

God wants to manifest His glory in your life so you can walk away from reading this book and from this encounter together in the Spirit, free, as free as a bird.

I say again: You can walk away free today!

I feel in my spirit that the Holy Spirit has a prophetic word of encouragement for you right now. This is what I feel the Spirit of the Lord is saying: For God is not a man that He should lie, neither is He like the sons of men that He should change His mind, has He not said it, and will He not do it! For God has purposed and established within Himself; yes God has sworn by Himself, He has established an eternal oath of covenant, and on the basis of that eternal covenant that cannot and will not be broken He desires to minister to everyone, but especially to those who believe. Yes, He desires to confirm the truth of His word to those with an ear of faith, so those who have an ear to hear, those who have an ear of faith, take heed and listen in order to receive from God; in order to take that step and enter into His provision made available on your behalf and for your life.

Right now I want to pray with those of you who have need, and I ask you to **receive** your deliverance; to **receive** that deliverance for whatever area of your life you have been held in bondage. I encourage you to take that opportunity right now to **receive.**

So come in agreement with me as I pray for you and I declare over you in Jesus Name: **Father God, in Jesus name, WE BRAKE THAT YOKE! And Holy Spirit, we ask You *to cause these people to walk away totally free and liberated,* and we trust You for it, right now! Thank you God! Thank you for your power we engage by faith right now! Amen!**

If your life has changed as a result of reading this book, or if you have received a miracle as a result of my prayer for you, please write to me and let me know.

I would love to share your joy, so that my joy in writing this book may be full!

Let me also encourage you to get yourself a copy of *"The Mirror Bible"* available online at www.Amazon.com and several other book sellers. It is the best paraphrased version of the New Testament Scriptures, translated from the original Greek text, *which I have ever read!*

In closing let me just say that if you want me or someone who is part of our team to come to where you are, anywhere in the world, and give a talk or teach you and some of your friends about the gospel message and this magnificent work of redemption, simply contact us at www.LivingWordIntl.com, or you can always find me on Facebook.

"That which was from the beginning,

which we have heard
(with our spiritual ears),
which we have seen
(with our spiritual eyes),
which we have looked upon
**(beheld, focused our
attention upon)**,
and which our hands have also
handled
**(which we have also
experienced)**,

concerning the Word of life,

we declare to you,

that you also may have
this fellowship with us;

and truly our fellowship is
with the Father
and with His Son Jesus
Christ.

And these things we write to you
that your joy may be full."
~ 1John 1:1-4

About the Author

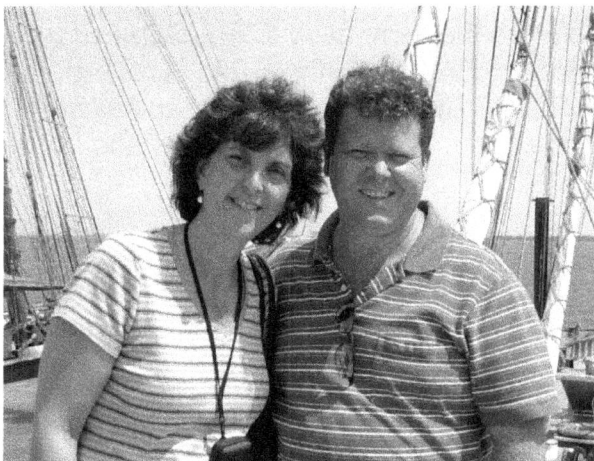

Rudi & Carmen Louw together oversee: Living Word International.

They also travel and minister both locally and internationally.

Rudi was born and raised in the country of South Africa, while Carmen grew up in Cortland, New York.

They function in the ministry of reconciliation (2 Corinthians 5:18-21) and flow strongly with the Holy Spirit and His anointing to teach, preach, prophesy, heal, and whatever is needed to touch people's lives with the reality of God's love and power.

God has given them keen insight into what He has to say to mankind in the work of redemption concerning the revelation and restoration of humanity's true identity.

Therefore they emphasize THE GOSPEL, IN CHRIST REALITIES, the GRACE of God, the WORD OF RIGHTEOUSNESS, *and all such eternal truths essential to salvation and living the CHRIST-LIFE.*

They have been granted this wisdom and revelation into the knowledge of God by the resurrected Spirit of Jesus Christ, *to establish and strengthen believers in the faith of God, and to activate them in ministering to others.*

Not only are people set free from the poison and bondage of sin, condemnation and all kinds of intimidation, (upheld, strengthened and reinforced by age old religious ideas born out of ignorance) **but many are brought into a closer more intimate relationship with Father God, as Daddy**, through accurate teaching and unveiling of the gospel message, prophetic words, healings and miracles.

Rudi & Carmen are closely knitted together with many other effective Christians, church fellowships, and groups of believers who share the same revelation and passion **to impart the truth of the gospel to others, so as to impact and transform the world we live in with the LOVE and POWER of God.**

www.ingramcontent.com/pod-product-compliance
Lightning Source LLC
Chambersburg PA
CBHW060758050426
42449CB00008B/1444